The New Teacher Survival Kit

MATT BROMLEY

Published by Spark Books UK

M J Bromley

Published by Spark Education Books UK
Twitter: @SparkBooksUK

Published in 2017
© Bromley Education 2017

ISBN-13: 978-1542815932
ISBN-10: 1542815932

M J Bromley

The New Teacher Survival Kit

Contents

Introduction

Tricks and treats

I bought a Border collie pup recently and, at eight weeks, have just begun training her. I don't want to sound disparaging but the experience reminded me a lot of my newly qualified teacher (NQT) year.

I've christened my dog Meg in the sheep farmer's tradition of using a mono-syllabic name that lends itself to constant repetition. Besides, I wanted a name I could holler around the village without being embarrassed - (I've recently had to beckon our friend's Shitzu, Buttons, and can still hear the echo of my neighbours' laughter.)

The very first Border collie, Old Hemp, had a mother called Meg so the name has a rich heritage. But it's already wearing thin. I use her name so many times a day - a crescendo rising from loving come-hither to firm command to angry chastisement - that the sound of it is beginning to lose all meaning for me.

Meg is, as I say, a Border collie - a breed well known for their social skills, eagerness to please, intelligence and boundless energy. But every coin has a flip-side and Meg's propensity to be social also means she doesn't like being left alone and cries through the night keeping me awake, her eagerness to please can translate as an over-zealous tendency to bite the children, chase the cats and herd the rabbits, her intelligence means she is quick-witted, often one step ahead of me as she sneaks into the food cupboard, and her boundless energy makes her tireless but me exhausted as I try to keep up.

Our training regime started by using Meg's name as often as possible - always 'Meg', just 'Meg' (no silly nicknames like our pets and children usually acquire as soon as they leave the womb) and always enunciated clearly followed by a pregnant pause to gain her attention before a command is given.

Next, I taught her to 'sit' using a simple one-word command

accompanied by a hand gesture, plus a treat as a reward the first few times she succeeded. The real secret to this obedience trick was repetition and then positive reinforcement. I kept doing it and whenever she got it right, I gave her a treat and made a fuss of her so she knew she'd done what I wanted her to do and to do it again next time. It took patience and determination but it worked.

I had drafted a list of one-word commands and their accompanying hand gestures before Meg had arrived and shared them with my family so we were consistent in the words and body language we used with our puppy the moment she crossed the threshold, thereby avoiding any confusion or mixed messages. Again, simplicity, consistency and repetition were key - plus plenty of praise.

On the morning of day two of our training she learnt to "sit", "stay" and "come". I was over the moon with her progress and considered myself the natural heir to Barbara Woodhouse. On the afternoon of day two she learnt to wee on the carpet, chew the legs off the sofa, and bite the legs of my daughter. I considered myself the natural heir to Barbara Windsor, screaming: "Get outta my house!"

It was a game of two halves, shall we say.

And that is why training my dog reminds me of training to be a teacher: it is full of highs and lows. Sometimes the good advice I read in books and on the Internet works; sometimes it does not. Sometimes things go my way; sometimes they do not. Sometimes I am a picture of patience and calm; sometimes I bop her on the nose and shout at her, then feel utterly remorseful when she stares at me with her puppy-dog eyes (never has that phrase meant so much).

Sometimes Meg is obedient and attentive, quick to pick things up and respond; sometimes she is tired, hungry, naughty, bored, distracted, incontinent, and noisy. Sometimes I am the best teacher and she is the best pupil; sometimes we are neither of us these things.

Sound familiar? I think I may just have described life, love and teacher-training. Meg and I live and breathe, we think and feel. We get tired and hungry, we get bored and irritable.

Thus is life. And that is what being a trainee-teacher, a newly qualified teacher, a recently qualified teacher, and - for that matter - an experienced teacher - is like. Get used to it and get over it.

That might sound harsh but consider it a bit of well-intentioned tough love with which to start this book: as you get to grips with teaching and reflect on lessons gone by, don't be too hard on yourself for the times when it didn't go your way - just learn from it. The one thing I can guarantee about your early years in teaching is that you will continue to make mistakes and you will continue to learn from them - and isn't that just great? Life's a lesson! We all make mistakes and sometimes the mistakes are not yours to make anyway. Sometimes they are not even mistakes. Sometimes, your pupils are being disobedient because they are tired or hungry. Sometimes the advice you followed that didn't work out was bad advice or not appropriate for your context.

As you embark on your career as a qualified teacher, don't expect perfection, don't expect a summer transformation whereby all your early follies and foibles will fall away and you emerge from your chrysalis a beautiful butterfly unrecognisable from the caterpillar you once were. Rome - to coin a cliché - wasn't built in a day and nor will your teaching practice.

It will - hence the name teaching *practice* - take years of trial and error and even then you will never perfect it. You will have to keep on trying to get better at teaching until you retire or die (to paraphrase the Eliza Doolittle-like Dylan Wiliam).

Teaching is a physically and emotionally demanding job that involves hours of standing and listening and talking. It is intellectually demanding because you have to plan to meet the needs of pupils with a wide range of starting points and from a wide range of backgrounds, and you have to look afresh at a subject you know inside out but from a novice pupil's point of view. Teaching can involve working with vulnerable and distressed pupils, as well as calming angry and uncooperative ones; it can involve challenging complacent pupils and encouraging insecure ones. And then there's the parents.

But teaching is also the best job in the world. Teaching is an honour and a joy. There can be few jobs more crucial to society and few careers that offer such rich rewards. You have the privilege of shaping young minds and watching your pupils grow into intelligent, responsible citizens.

Teaching is tough, of course, but it is tough because it matters; it is tough because you are doing something important, you are improving the world around you one person at a time.

A friend of mine is a nurse and when she's asked what she does for a living she replies (albeit tongue in cheek) "I save lives". Take her lead: now that you're a teacher, the next time you're asked what you do for a living, say "I change lives". It's hyperbole, yes, it's gilding the lily, of course – but it is also fundamentally true.

Because you do. You do have the best job in the world and you do change lives. Each and every day. You do a job which many other people could and would not do. So enjoy it, you deserve it and you have earned it.

Part One

Being a teacher

Chapter One

Taking your first steps

Teaching is tough. At times it might feel like you're spinning lots of plates and, if you're not careful, the result could resemble a Greek wedding.

The trick to keeping all those plates spinning is to break down what can be a complex, multi-faceted job into each of its constituent parts, to deconstruct the whole and identify its components then reconstruct it again one piece at a time.

In practice, this means creating a checklist of short-term, manageable tasks. To help you get started, here are seven jobs to tick off the list as soon as you start a new teaching job...

1. Find your bearings

Try to learn the layout of the school – perhaps by studying a floor plan (there's usually one in the school handbook or prospectus). If you get time during the day, do a walkabout around the school buildings to familiarise yourself with them.

Find out where the main facilities are, such as the toilets, the staffroom, the hall, the canteen, the school office, and the photocopying machine.

2. Learn your timetable

You will need to become familiar – and quickly - with the timing of the school day and with your timetable of lessons.

Timetables vary considerably from school to school, so find out and memorise what time the school day starts and finishes, how long lessons are, how long breaks are, whether there is a daily or weekly assembly and when this takes place.

3. Read the school handbook and policies

Ask for and read the school prospectus, staff handbook and main policies and procedures. It will prove especially useful to read about the school rules and the whole-school behaviour policy – you will need to adhere to it at all times. Another policy for your urgent attention is the one on safeguarding and child protection.

4. Establish who's who

Find out the names of key members of staff, especially the designated lead for child protection.

You should also identify a couple of senior managers in case you need to refer a pupil. Make a real effort to get to know the staff in the office as well as the caretaking staff and reprographics staff – they will be invaluable allies! Clerical and support people know a lot about the way that the school is run, and they can make your life much easier.

5. Get to know the staffroom...with caution

The staffroom should be a place of solace and succour but, a word of warning, approach it with caution initially and be careful where you sit!

Although staffrooms are becoming less territorial than they used to be, some teachers can still be precious about their favourite chairs. Before you take a seat, ask 'is it ok to sit here?' This might seem silly to you right now, but just wait until you've got a full-time teaching job and you find a trainee or 'newbie' in your own favourite seat in the staffroom next to all your closest colleagues to whom you need to offload.

For the first days, don't be too vocal in the staffroom, be polite and friendly. Laugh at people's jokes, join in with conversations. Slowly come out of your shell when you have felt the lay of the land and your new colleagues have got the measure of you, too!

Here are some more helpful hints to ensure you make friends and influence people in the staffroom...

Use your own mug

If you commit the cardinal sin of taking someone else's mug, be prepared for the backlash. It has been known for the entire morning break to be taken up with staff deep in conversation over missing cups, who has got them, where they were last placed, how could someone mistake their cup for someone else's and so on.

Wash your cup up after you've used it

If you do have to commit that cardinal sin of using someone's else's mug, at least have the decency of washing it up afterwards…don't twist the knife in the heart of your victim by leaving their beloved possession abandoned and filthy in the sink. Leave it in a pristine condition and put it back in its rightful place.

Always make a fuss of anyone who's been off sick, even if it is only for one day

It is always good manners to find out how people are feeling when they have been off sick, but in the staffroom, this often takes on a dramatic level. Heartfelt enquiries about a person's well-being accompanied by pale, concerned faces, and hugs are common types of behaviour.

Don't take the last slice of cake

Most schools have at least one day of the week when treats are kindly brought in for staff. Though you will look longingly at the final slice of mouth-wateringly delicious chocolate cake sitting temptingly on the plate, don't make the fatal mistake of eating it. If you do, the whole of the staffroom will gang up to play the longest game of 'Whodunit?' you've ever seen.

6. Impress in staff meetings

School staff meetings can be daunting so here are some tips for how to handle them…

There will be an agenda for most meetings and you should receive a copy in advance. Always try to read it beforehand. Remember that every item offers you a chance to learn something new, so draw on your expertise and research the background so you know what your colleagues are talking about.

Find out what kind of meeting you're attending – is it a short staff briefing (key messages given by senior leaders) or a presentation (usually with slides), or is it a committee meeting in which you'll work as part of a team?

Be an active listener, ask questions where appropriate and seek clarification on key points. In a committee meeting, don't say too much. Occasionally, try to share your unique expertise – after all, NQTs and new teachers are supposed to be au fait with current theory having more recently been trained.

If refreshments are available volunteer to serve them to those present – it will give you a chance to speak to everyone.

You probably won't agree with everything you hear in staff meetings, but stay calm and keep your counsel. Try not to react on the basis of right and wrong – keep asking yourself what you can learn from what is being said. Stay with the facts and keep the emotions under control.

Remember that - rightly or wrongly - staff meetings serve social as well as professional purposes. They can help with team building, but they can also give you – the newcomer – a very valuable insight into group dynamics. Be vigilant at all times and watch people's body language. Remember that you are also trying to establish your identity within the team. Be modest, though suitably assertive when you need to be and always show that you are willing to learn and contribute. As such, be aware of your own body language – it can say more about you than any words you say. Smile and make plenty of eye contact.

7. Succeed at parents' evenings

Manners cost nothing – as you greet parents, stand up, smile and shake hands. Thank them for coming. Ask them how the journey was. These simple things make relationships possible.

The parent may have been dragged from teacher to teacher to be told some pretty depressing things or, at the least, may be tired and bombarded with information. Be the surprise. Make some comment about how well their son or daughter is doing. Give them a reason to believe you can see all sides of the child.

But… you also have to be honest. Tell the parent that you need their help getting the situation back on track, and you want their son or daughter to do as well as they possibly can. Say what needs to be said but in such a way that suggests you're not disgusted with the child but believe change is possible.

Here are a few other tips to help you adjust to life as a teacher:

- Become familiar with the key policies that will affect you, such as behaviour, homework, child protection, and health and safety. Review your practices to ensure you are meeting these policies.
- Make a note of the general work ethic in the school. Arrive on time and leave when the majority of staff do.
- Discuss your job description with your head of department and/or induction mentor. Make sure you know what's expected of you.
- Be courteous and attentive to others, and always listen to advice from colleagues.
- Talk a little about yourself, but not too much, and don't keep going on about what you did in your last school, during your teaching practice, or before you became a teacher.
- Do not rock the boat too soon. Even if you have an innovative idea, wait until you have established a credible reputation and some positive rapport with colleagues before proposing a change, no matter how small.
- Mind your meeting manners. There are unofficial guidelines that dictate decorum during meetings – read the runes as quickly as possible or ask someone to give you the inside track.

Chapter Two

Surviving and thriving each term

Whilst getting to grips with your new job - which we have already said is complex and multi-faceted, and therefore daunting and demanding - you should be careful not to overwork yourself or become stressed. Teaching might be the best job in the world but it is still only a *job*. You must not allow it to take over your life, certainly not at the expense of your health and wellbeing. Rather, you should strive to strike a healthy work-life balance. Here are some tips to help you do just that...

1. Just say no

Your colleagues may still regard you as a keen newbie and they may look to you as a natural volunteer whenever something needs doing. But you need to manage your workload and strike some semblance of work-life balance if you are to be effective and survive. You must not spread yourself too thinly or try conquer the world overnight, no matter how much you wish to please or impress and no matter how eager you are to learn new things and add to your CV. It's not a sign of weakness to say no.

2. Manage your marking

Written feedback is important and it does make a difference. But it is not a panacea and must not take over your life. As with all things, moderation is the key. Try to keep your written feedback succinct and meaningful - perhaps establish some form of shorthand, maybe symbols, and consider using stamps or stickers for this. Manage the amount of work you mark - perhaps marking one piece of work every five lessons with pupils engaging in self and peer assessment in-between. You could set tasks for pupils to respond to your feedback so that the time you do spend marking is time well spent.

3. Be discerning

Teachers have a tendency to be magpies and yet I would caution you against trying to adopt every new pedagogic fad in your classroom during your first few years. You should read and research widely and be willing to take risks and try new things. But you should always approach new ideas with an open mind and test them with a class before adopting them as your new default teaching style. Also, you must be careful that trying new strategies doesn't cause you additional stress or add to your workload, or indeed confuse your pupils thus hampering the learning environment and their outcomes.

4. Know your school

You are part of a school community - a cohort of pupils, parents, staff, governors and others who have a stake in your school's success. You should get to know your school as soon as possible - and all aspects of it. The more you know and the more active you are, the easier you will find your job. Your colleagues will come to know and respect you better and your pupils and parents will come to regard you as a part of their school with an investment in its future, not just someone passing through.

To do this, you should get involved in events outside your own subject and in after school activities and open evenings. Another easy way to 'fit in' is simply to spend time in the staffroom talking to colleagues over coffee. Don't work in a silo - as tempting as it is to stay in your classroom at break and lunchtime preparing for your next lesson, it's important to get out and talk to staff about the pupils you teach and to switch off and socialise. Talking of which...

5. Ask for help

If you need help then ask for it - you are not alone. Your head teacher, head of department and other colleagues are there to support you so use them. You are part of a teaching profession and it is so called because it is a collective enterprise. Invite colleagues into your classroom to see you teach and ask for their feedback. Ask your colleagues if you can observe them, too, so you can learn from their practice. You will have a wealth of skills and experience in your own school and won't always need to go on training courses to develop your knowledge. What's more, rather than listening to generic theory, you can go sit at the back of a class to watch how another teacher manages the same pupils you actually teach.

6. Develop yourself

One of the Teachers' Standards requires that NQTs and recently qualified teachers can show a commitment to improving their practice through appropriate professional development. This emphasis on taking responsibility for your own professional development is a key element of the expectations of teachers as professionals.

It is implied that you should: care about your own professional growth and development; have objectives and plan for the professional skills you need now and in the future to do your job well; and have expectations that the school you work for will facilitate and enhance your professional development, and demonstrate a positive attitude to your professional future in teaching.

So make sure you and your school honour your rights - take care to develop yourself. You will be busy and it is all too easy to get stuck in a vicious cycle of lesson planning, delivery and marking, but don't neglect your professional development. Make sure you are given time and space to reflect on your professional needs and to learn new skills and knowledge.

7. Look after yourself

Perhaps more important than developing yourself, though, is looking after yourself. Nurturing your body, mind and soul is vital if you are to get the most out of your early years of teaching and survive intact. If you look after your health and well-being, you are more likely to be an effective, happy teacher. So don't give up on sport and exercise and don't stop socialising. As well as helping you to switch off, it will defuse your anxiety. Another good tip for relieving stress is to make time for eating sensibly and to get plenty of sleep. In short, don't let teaching absorb all of your time.

Be realistic - you are not a superhero and you are not the only teacher in the school so don't expect to be the one to help every single pupil. Similarly, don't set unrealistic expectations for yourself when you break for the holidays - as tempting as it is to promise yourself you'll catch up on all the housework. You need to set aside quality time to relax and unwind.

And finally…

8. Good is good enough

I know this might sound like the 'soft bigotry of low expectations' much criticised by the former Education Secretary Michael Gove but, whilst having high expectations of yourself and your teaching is clearly admirable, there's a fine line between *high* expectations and *unrealistic* expectations. Newly qualified teachers and teachers starting jobs in new schools often make the mistake of thinking that every lesson has to be akin to a New Year's Eve firework extravaganza and as a consequence each lesson takes ten times longer to plan than it does to teach. What's more, the quality of learning is compromised because pupils are over-excited by the engaging and interactive activities - which often detract from the learning or are divorced from real learning - before you've fully established the foundations, the rules and routines that will foster a positive learning environment. Plus, pupils come to expect whizz-bang lessons all year round and you simply can't sustain that.

This approach invariably leads to bad behaviour or, at the very least, slower rates of progress. So try to plan and teach 'good' rather than 'outstanding' lessons whilst you build some solid foundations and save the fireworks for New Year's Eve. Make your explanations quick and clear, don't let anyone talk over you. Don't use too many unnecessary questions if you don't care about the answers - questioning should be used for assessment, it won't make your teaching any more interesting but it might slow it down. Don't be afraid to repeat yourself if you think somebody isn't listening. Remember you are passing on information or giving an explanation - you are not performing on stage at the Comedy Store. Try not to plan activities that rely on pupils' goodwill or compliance until you know them well enough to know you can count on it.

Chapter Three

Passing your induction Year

In order to be a successful teacher, you will have to demonstrate how you are meeting the national Teachers' Standards which are a set of professional behaviours and duties all teachers in England are expected to adhere to. The Teachers' Standards are particularly important to new teachers because they form the basis of the targets you have to meet in order to pass your induction year.

We'll take a look at what you're expected to do during your induction year - and at the support you're entitled to in return - towards the end of this chapter but first let's look at the Teachers' Standards in more detail…

The Teachers' Standards

Why were the standards introduced?

The Teachers' Standards were introduced in 2012 and replaced the standards for qualified teacher status (QTS) and the core professional standards previously published by the Training and Development Agency for Schools (TDA), as well as the General Teaching Council for England's Code of Conduct and Practice for Registered Teachers.

The standards apply to the vast majority of teachers regardless of their career stage. The Teachers' Standards apply to: trainees working towards QTS; all teachers completing their statutory induction period; and those covered by the new performance appraisal arrangements.

Part Two of the Teachers' Standards, which relates to professional and personal conduct, is used to assess cases of serious misconduct, regardless of the sector in which a teacher works.

The standards define the minimum level of practice expected of trainees and teachers from the point of being awarded QTS.

Head teachers (or appraisers) should assess your performance against the standards to a level that is consistent with what should reasonably be expected of you in the relevant role and at the relevant stage of your career (whether you are a newly qualified teacher (NQT), a mid-career teacher, or a more experienced practitioner).

The professional judgment of head teachers and appraisers is therefore central to appraisal against the standards.

The standards were designed to set out a basic framework within which all teachers should operate from the point of initial qualification. Appropriate self-evaluation, reflection and professional development activity is critical to improving your practice at all career stages.

The standards set out clearly the key areas in which you should be able to assess your own practice, and receive feedback from colleagues. As your careers progress, you will be expected to extend the depth and breadth of knowledge, skill and understanding that you demonstrate in meeting the standards, as is judged to be appropriate to the role you are fulfilling and the context in which you are working.

What are the standards?

Set high expectations which inspire, motivate and challenge pupils

- establish a safe and stimulating environment for pupils, rooted in mutual respect
- set goals that stretch and challenge pupils of all backgrounds, abilities and dispositions
- demonstrate consistently the positive attitudes, values and behaviour which are expected of pupils.

Promote good progress and outcomes by pupils

- be accountable for pupils' attainment, progress and outcomes
- be aware of pupils' capabilities and their prior knowledge, and plan teaching to build on these

- guide pupils to reflect on the progress they have made and their emerging needs
- demonstrate knowledge and understanding of how pupils learn and how this impacts on teaching
- encourage pupils to take a responsible and conscientious attitude to their own work and study.

Demonstrate good subject and curriculum knowledge

- have a secure knowledge of the relevant subject(s) and curriculum areas, foster and maintain pupils' interest in the subject, and address misunderstandings
- demonstrate a critical understanding of developments in the subject and curriculum areas, and promote the value of scholarship
- demonstrate an understanding of and take responsibility for promoting high standards of literacy, articulacy and the correct use of standard English, whatever the teacher's specialist subject
- if teaching early reading, demonstrate a clear understanding of systematic synthetic phonics
- if teaching early mathematics, demonstrate a clear understanding of appropriate teaching strategies.

Plan and teach well-structured lessons

- impart knowledge and develop understanding through effective use of lesson time
- promote a love of learning and children's intellectual curiosity
- set homework and plan other out-of-class activities to consolidate and extend the knowledge and understanding pupils have acquired
- reflect systematically on the effectiveness of lessons and approaches to teaching
- contribute to the design and provision of an engaging curriculum within the relevant subject area(s).

Adapt teaching to respond to the strengths and needs of all pupils

- know when and how to differentiate appropriately, using approaches which enable pupils to be taught effectively

- have a secure understanding of how a range of factors can inhibit pupils' ability to learn, and how best to overcome these
- demonstrate an awareness of the physical, social and intellectual development of children, and know how to adapt teaching to support pupils' education at different stages of development
- have a clear understanding of the needs of all pupils, including those with special educational needs; those of high ability; those with English as an additional language; those with disabilities; and be able to use and evaluate distinctive teaching approaches to engage and support them.

Make accurate and productive use of assessment
- know and understand how to assess the relevant subject and curriculum areas, including statutory assessment requirements
- make use of formative and summative assessment to secure pupils' progress
- use relevant data to monitor progress, set targets, and plan subsequent lessons
- give pupils regular feedback, both orally and through accurate marking, and encourage pupils to respond to the feedback.

Manage behaviour effectively to ensure a good and safe learning environment
- have clear rules and routines for behaviour in classrooms, and take responsibility for promoting good and courteous behaviour both in classrooms and around the school, in accordance with the school's behaviour policy
- have high expectations of behaviour, and establish a framework for discipline with a range of strategies, using praise, sanctions and rewards consistently and fairly
- manage classes effectively, using approaches which are appropriate to pupils' needs in order to involve and motivate them
- maintain good relationships with pupils, exercise appropriate authority, and act decisively when necessary.

Fulfil wider professional responsibilities
- make a positive contribution to the wider life and ethos of the

school
- develop effective professional relationships with colleagues, knowing how and when to draw on advice and specialist support
- deploy support staff effectively
- take responsibility for improving teaching through appropriate professional development, responding to advice and feedback from colleagues
- communicate effectively with parents with regard to pupils' achievements and well-being.

In addition, there is a set of standards relating to the personal and professional conduct of teachers which state that:

Teachers uphold public trust in the profession and maintain high standards of ethics and behaviour, within and outside school, by:
- treating pupils with dignity, building relationships rooted in mutual respect, and at all times observing proper boundaries appropriate to a teacher's professional position
- having regard for the need to safeguard pupils' well-being, in accordance with statutory provisions
- showing tolerance of and respect for the rights of others
- not undermining fundamental British values, including democracy, the rule of law, individual liberty and mutual respect, and tolerance of those with different faiths and beliefs
- ensuring that personal beliefs are not expressed in ways which exploit pupils' vulnerability or might lead them to break the law.

Teachers must have proper and professional regard for the ethos, policies and practices of the school in which they teach, and maintain high standards in their own attendance and punctuality.

Teachers must have an understanding of, and always act within, the statutory frameworks which set out their professional duties and responsibilities.

The induction year

Having passed your teacher-training qualification, you will be expected to work an induction year. This is a probationary period during which you will be supported by your head teacher and a mentor (usually someone from your department who understands your subject specialism) and be observed several times in order to ensure that your teaching is of a sufficiently high standard to be awarded Qualified Teacher Status and be offered a permanent contract.

So what, exactly, are you expected to do during your induction..?

As a new teacher, you are expected to:

- meet with your induction tutor to discuss and agree priorities for your induction and keep these priorities under constant review;
- agree with your induction tutor how best to use your reduced timetable allowance;
- provide evidence of your progress against The Teachers' Standards;
- participate fully in the agreed monitoring and development programme;
- raise any concerns with your induction tutor as soon as practicable;
- consult your appropriate body named contact at an early stage if there are or may be difficulties in resolving issues with your tutor/within the institution;
- keep track of and participate effectively in the scheduled classroom observations, progress reviews and formal assessment meetings;
- agree with your induction tutor the start and end dates of the induction period/part periods and the dates of any absences from work during any period/part period; and
- retain copies of all assessment forms.

An induction is not a one-sided process, however. In exchange for doing all of the above, you are entitled to receive support from your head teacher and mentor. So what support can you expect?

Your head teacher/principal is, along with the appropriate body, jointly responsible for monitoring, supporting and assessing you during your induction, and should:

- ensure the induction tutor is appropriately trained and has sufficient time to carry out their role effectively;
- ensure an appropriate and personalised induction programme is in place;
- ensure your progress is reviewed regularly, including through observations and feedback of your teaching;
- ensure that termly assessments are carried out and reports completed and sent to the appropriate body;
- maintain and retain accurate records of employment that will count towards the induction period;
- make the governing body aware of the arrangements, that have been put in place to support your induction;
- make a recommendation to the appropriate body on whether your performance against The Teachers' Standards is satisfactory or requires an extension;
- participate appropriately in the appropriate body's quality assurance procedures; and retain all relevant documentation/evidence/forms on file for six years.

Your induction mentor, meanwhile, should:

- provide, or co-ordinate, guidance and effective support including coaching and mentoring for your professional development (with the appropriate body where necessary);
- carry out regular progress reviews throughout the induction period;
- undertake three formal assessment meetings during the total induction period co-ordinating input from other colleagues as appropriate (normally three termly, or pro-rata for part-time staff);
- inform you during the assessment if you are meeting the judgments to be recorded in the formal assessment record and invite you to add your comments;
- ensure that your teaching is observed and feedback provided;
- ensure you are aware of how, both within and outside the institution, you can raise any concerns about your induction programme or your personal progress; and

- take prompt, appropriate action if you appear to be having difficulties.

Part Two

First Impressions Count

Chapter Four

Developing a presence in the classroom

As a new teacher in a new school you need to establish a presence. One way to do this by 'owning your classroom space'. For example, you can teach from the back of the classroom, kneel or crouch down between desks or at the front of the room, sit at a desk, on the floor or on a chair or table, and you can try entering the pupils' physical space by sitting next to them, leaning on their desks, walking slowly between desks.

You can also use your physical presence such as standing in a grounded way - finding your 'centre' and standing with your feet apart and your knees bent slightly. You can lengthen your spine, stand as if your head is being pulled up by a string. You can release tension by swinging your arms from your shoulders. You can calm your breathing by raising your arms slowly as you breathe in, and then bring them down again while exhaling and making a "ssshh" sound.

You can think about eye contact – aim to look open and receptive. Make eye contact with your pupils. You can use gestures to punctuate what you say and move around in the space if you want to create a bigger presence. This helps you to appear strong and confident. You can create an aura around yourself by staying still and casting a net around the room with your eyes.

You can also use your voice in order to establish your presence. For example, you can breathe in and hold for three seconds. As you breathe out, project your voice and say the days of the week; then try the months; then the alphabet. This helps you to speak from the chest, not from the back of the throat. To seem authoritative, practise your breathing to find your "home note" – your own distinctive voice – from your chest.

Once you've set upon the tone of voice and body language that best suits you and projects authority, and once you feel as if you 'own' your space, think about the principles on which you want to run your room. For example, three principles on which I operate my room (and which you may wish to adopt) are: openness, consistency and fairness. If you do take these, make them your own and communicate them as often as possible both explicitly and implicitly through the way you speak and the actions you take...

The three pillars of an effective classroom

1. Openness

It is important that your rules are known and understood, that every pupil in your class knows what is expected of them and understands the consequences they are likely to face should they fail to live up to those expectations. Ideally, pupils should be involved in the process of drawing up the rules or at least be consulted once they've been drawn up. It is important that your pupils feel your rules are reasonable and appropriate. Personally, I favour using a pupil contract which acts in much the same way as an employment contract: it states what is expected of pupils and what they can expect in return from the school. If pupils sign it, they feel like adults; moreover, they feel that they have some ownership, they feel duty-bound to obey the rules. I use a pupil contract which has two columns: one for the pupil, one for the teacher. The two columns should be evenly balanced – for every expectation you have of your pupils, you the teacher should do something in return. For example, if you expect pupils to complete homework on time, is it not also fair that you mark that work within a reasonable timescale? pupils see this balanced contract, not only as fair (because their teacher does not expect anything of pupils that they are not prepared to do themselves), but also as a step towards the world of work (because their teacher does not expect anything of pupils that will not be expected of them when they get a job). A contract is about responsibilities - showing pupils that, with rights, comes responsibility - rather than about being told what they can and can't do. Therefore, it becomes enabling rather than restricting. The contract, once agreed, needs to be articulated to pupils and referred to as often as possible.

2. Consistency

It is important that your rules are (or appear to be) applied consistently: the rules - and the authority and respect of the teacher applying them - will be undermined if one person is punished for an offence whilst someone else, committing the same offence, escapes punishment or is punished differently. This is not to say that every pupil is the same and should be treated the same. But pupils and parents are likely to dispute the punishment you give (and feel they have the right to appeal) if they feel that their son or daughter has been made an example of or has been unfairly treated. Often, this is simply about effective communication: explaining what has happened, what action you have taken and why you think that action is appropriate (in other words, explain your rationale and explain how your decision is consistent with similar cases), and what will happen next.

3. Fairness

It is important that your class rules are applied fairly, that everyone in your classroom feels they are treated justly. In practice, this means allowing everyone a right of reply. It is sensible to listen to a range of different opinions before taking action and to involve the 'offender' in the process of agreeing the consequences for his/her actions. Often, a situation arises because a pupil feels ignored. They are told off for something they did not do and are not allowed to explain. They grow agitated by this and can become confrontational. The best thing the teacher can do when trying to resolve the situation is allow the pupil the time and space to calm down then listen to them; allow the pupil to have their say without interruption. This does not mean contradicting the rules or what another teacher or pupil has said, nor does it mean being 'soft'. It means being human, being the adult, being fair. Once you have listened to the pupil's point of view, explain how others may perceive the incident, ask the pupil to put themselves in other people's shoes for a moment. Explain that you, as a teacher, also have to abide by rules and you too would face consequences if you broke them. By getting the pupil to see that he or she is not so different from their teacher you are again reinforcing the idea of fairness.

*

In addition to openness, consistency and fairness, these general principles are also worth bearing in mind when applying behaviour management strategies:

1. All young people enjoy being effectively rewarded; your rewards system must motivate pupils to do their best;

2. Most young people are responsible for their own behaviour but need clear guidelines of what constitutes acceptable behaviour if they are to accept the consequences of their misbehaviour;

3. Effective communication between teachers, parents/carers and pupils is essential; your school's behaviour policy must be published and understood by parents and pupils;

4. Work/activities must be matched to pupils' abilities; work must be differentiated so that more-able pupils are challenged and less-able pupils are supported;

5. You and your support staff must be trained and supported so that you act in a way which is consistent and fair and so you are not left vulnerable and exposed;

6. Robust procedures must be in place for the minority of pupils who consistently misbehave in order to protect other pupils and ensure learning is not affected – this means knowing and applying the school's policies.

Chapter Five

Creating your learning environment

As well as developing a presence in your classroom and setting the principles on which you will run your room, you need to work hard to create a positive classroom environment which is conducive to learning. So what does this look like in practice..?

1. Seating plans

Every teacher has his or her own preference about whether to arrange desks in rows, groups or a horseshoe, and this will depend largely on the age of the children and what best suits the subject you are teaching. Having a seating plan is not only convenient for you as a teacher but may be welcomed by the pupils. Desks and tables should also be arranged so that pupils can move around safely. You also need to think about your desk – where is the best place for it to go?

2. Resources

If you are going into a class that has not been in regular use, it is possible that other teachers may have "borrowed" items from it. Check with colleagues who are teaching similar age groups or subjects about what you will need and equip your class similarly. Generally speaking, your head of department should supply you with all the essentials.

You are also likely to want to provide resources that go above and beyond the basics – the things that engage pupils' interests and keep them motivated. If you are a secondary subject specialist, try organisations that are relevant to your subject, many of which do free resources, posters and other materials.

The walls around an interactive whiteboard or other focal points in the classroom should be kept clear of distractions. However, this might be the place to put learning prompts – such as the letters of the alphabet for primary pupils or the periodic table in a secondary science lab – and a poster setting out class rules. When considering a wall display, choose things that are appropriate to the age group and subject, and that are linked to good learning.

3. Where should you stand?

Everyone has a side of their body that they will instinctively favour. So whether you are right- or left-handed, you need to be aware that you will tend to speak to the opposite side of the classroom. One way to get around this potential problem is to spend some time in your classroom prior to starting your job so you can try out different sides and see how the class looks from all corners of the room. This will help you to decide where to place yourself in order to be most visible and effective, while having a good view of all the pupils.

4. Developing a growth mindset culture

As a kid I wanted to become a cliché when I grew up so I bought a guitar and grew my hair. I successfully learnt all the chords but struggled to combine them in a meaningful way (perhaps I should've joined an experimental jazz band instead of churning out 1980s power ballads). When my dreams of rock stardom eventually withered on the vine, I turned my attention to mastering magic, then to conquering chess, and to all manner of other hobbies.

What all these childhood endeavours had in common was that I took it for granted that I'd have to work hard at them, I knew I'd have to practise endlessly and that I wouldn't become expert overnight. I played that old six-string till my fingers bled, readily accepting that improvement would be incremental.

Most of us feel this way about our interests. We know, for example, that to run a marathon we'd have to train hard for months beforehand. And yet when it comes to schooling – to mastering English or maths or science – we often forget the importance of hard work and practice. We assume that academic ability, that one's IQ, is somehow fixed, innate. We might not do it consciously, but we say things like "maths isn't his forte" or "she's not a natural artist". That's why most pupils who start the year in the bottom set, end the year in the bottom set. By creating a culture in which pupils believe that their abilities are preordained, and in which they are either good at a subject or not, we discourage them from taking risks, from making mistakes. After all, if ability is fixed, then if at first you don't succeed, you may as well give up.

Sir Ken Robinson argues that every child starts out willing to take a chance. If they don't know, they'll have a go; they're not frightened of being wrong, he says. However, he contends that by the time they are adults, most people have lost that capacity because in schools we regard mistakes as the worst thing you can make and we educate people out of their creative capacities.

In her book, Mindset, Dr Carol Dweck calls the belief that "your qualities are carved in stone" the 'fixed mindset'. But does it really have to be this way?

What if we applied the same mindset to schooling as we do to our hobbies and interests? What if we taught our pupils that, although people may differ in every which way – in their initial talents and aptitudes, interests, or temperaments – everyone can change and grow through application and experience? What if we instilled in our pupils what Dr Dweck calls the "growth mindset", the belief that "your basic qualities are things you can cultivate through your efforts"?

Even Alfred Binet, the inventor of the IQ test, believed that education and practice could bring about fundamental changes in intelligence. He said, in his book Major Ideas about Children, "a few modern philosophers assert that an individual's intelligence is a fixed quantity which cannot be increased. We must protest against this brutal pessimism … with practice, training, and above all, method, we become more intelligent than we were before".

Practice, training, and method – these three words uttered a century ago – remain the perfect definition of what the best teachers do. They provide a safe and secure environment in which all pupils can learn without fear of failure and in which all pupils can increase their intelligence with deliberate practice.

Here are five practical strategies which can help instil the growth mindset in your classroom...

- Use frequent formative feedback
- High levels of challenge for every pupil
- Explicitly welcome mistakes
- Engage in deliberate practice
- Reward effort not attainment

Let's take a look at these five strategies in turn...

Use frequent formative feedback

Dr Carol Dweck's research found that people with a fixed mindset "greatly mis-estimated their performance and their ability [whilst] people with the growth mindset were amazingly accurate".

Why should this be? Because, as Dr Dweck says: "If, like those with the growth mindset, you believe you can develop yourself, then you're open to accurate information about your current abilities, even if it's unflattering. What's more, if you're oriented towards learning, as they are, you need accurate information about your current abilities in order to learn effectively."

We should, therefore, ensure that our pupils are acutely aware of their strengths and areas for development. We should frequently assess our pupils and give them formative feedback so that they know what they do well and what they can do better. We should dedicate quality time in our lessons for our pupils to act on this feedback, to redraft work in order to improve upon it.

High levels of challenge for every pupil

Dr Dweck and Alfred Binet (the inventor of the IQ test) agree that everyone can improve with practice; they agree that effort is more important than 'talent' or 'innate ability'. Therefore, we must challenge our pupils to be the best, we must have high expectations of all our pupils and must encourage them to take a leap of faith, even if that means falling over a few times.

Teachers' attitudes directly affect their pupils' learning and, ultimately, the grades they get. A teacher who has high expectations of every pupil in his or her class will reap the rewards:

more pupils will rise to the challenge and succeed.

Many teachers think that lowering standards will give pupils a taste of success, boost their self-esteem, and raise their achievement. But all the evidence suggests it doesn't work. Instead, it leads to poorly educated children.

Instead, we should believe in the growth of the intellect and talent. We should set high standards for all our pupils, not just the ones who are already achieving.

Explicitly welcome mistakes

Teachers must actively encourage their pupils to make mistakes, they must foster a safe and secure environment in which falling over is not only accepted without criticism or humiliation, but in which it is actively encouraged as evidence of effective learning and of getting better at something.

Every teacher knows that some pupils do not raise their hands in class to answer a question because they fear they will be criticised or made to feel embarrassed for being wrong. And yet the opposite should be true: pupils should be eager to raise their hands because to get an answer wrong is to learn from their mistakes; to get an answer wrong is to learn the correct answer.

Equally, raising a hand to say, "I don't understand this … can you help?" is not a sign of weakness or low intelligence, it is a means of increasing one's intelligence.

Of course, making a mistake – even if you have a positive mindset – can be a painful experience. But a mistake shouldn't define you; it's a problem to be faced and learnt from. We teach this by modelling it, by publicly making mistakes and by making explicit our own implicit learning.

Engaging in deliberate practice

In his book, Outliers, Malcolm Gladwell suggests that as a society we value natural, effortless accomplishments over achievement through effort. We endow our heroes with superhuman abilities that lead them inevitably towards greatness. People with the growth mindset, however, believe something very different. For them, even geniuses have to work hard for their achievements. After all, what's heroic about having a gift?

Thomas Edison is credited with inventing the lightbulb but he wasn't an innate genius who single-handedly, effortlessly discovered his invention in – forgive the pun – a lightbulb moment. This is what Professor Anders Ericsson calls the iceberg effect: beneath the visible tip of genius, Edison had 30 assistants, including highly trained scientists, often working around the clock in a corporate-funded state-of-the-art laboratory.

'His' invention was the culmination of a lot of time-consuming work involving mathematicians, chemists, physicists, engineers and glass-blowers. Yes, he was a genius; but he wasn't born one. He was, according to his biography, an ordinary boy. He just worked hard, tried and tried again. He never stopped being curious, never shied away from taking on a new challenge.

Similar stories could be told of many geniuses such as Charles Darwin – whose Origin of Species was the result of years of research, a lot of effort and toil involving hundreds of discussions with colleagues and mentors, and went through several drafts, taking Darwin half a lifetime to finalise. In other words, his book wasn't created in the sweep of a god-like hand, it evolved slowly over time.

Jack Nicklaus, the most successful golfer of all time, famously said: "Nobody – but nobody – has ever become really proficient at golf without practice, without doing a lot of thinking and then hitting a lot of shots. It isn't so much a lack of talent; it's a lack of being able to repeat good shots consistently that frustrates most players. And the only answer to that is practice."

Matthew Syed, author of Bounce, quantifies the amount of "purposeful practice" that is required to achieve excellence. He says that "from art to science and from board games to tennis, it has been found that a minimum of 10 years is required to reach world-class status in any complex task".

Malcolm Gladwell, meanwhile, asserts that most top performers practise for around 1,000 hours per year. We should, therefore, provide our pupils with plenty of opportunities to practise and perfect their knowledge and skills.

Professor Daniel Willingham says that deliberate practice "reinforces [the] basic skills required for more advanced skills, it protects against forgetting, and improves transfer". Professor Siegfried Engelmann says that pupils need "five times more practice than many teachers expect".

There are two kinds of practice proven to be the most effective: first, distributed practice which is "a schedule of practice that spreads out study activities over time", and second, interleaved practice which is "a schedule of practice that mixes different kinds of problems, or a schedule of study that mixes different kinds of material, within a single study session" (Dunlosky et al, 2013).

Reward effort not attainment

Dr Dweck conducted research with hundreds of pupils. She gave each pupil a set of 10 problems to solve from a non-verbal IQ test. Most of the pupils did well and when they'd finished, she praised some of the pupils for their ability ("you got a high score, you must be smart") and some for their effort ("you got a high score, you must have worked hard").

Both groups were exactly equal to begin with but, after receiving praise, they began to differ. The pupils whose ability was praised were pushed into the fixed mindset. When they were given a choice, they rejected a challenging new task that they could learn from, favouring more of the same instead because they didn't want to do anything which would expose flaws in their intelligence and bring their talent into question. In contrast, 90 per cent of the pupils whose effort was praised wanted to try the challenging new task precisely because they could learn from it.

Dr Dweck concluded that praising ability actually lowered pupils' IQs whereas praising effort raised them. She also said that praising children's intelligence harmed their motivation because, although children love to be praised, especially for their talents, as soon as they hit a snag their confidence goes out of the window and their motivation hits rock bottom. If success means they're smart, then failure means they're dumb.

This doesn't mean we shouldn't praise children, Dr Dweck argues. But it does mean we should only use a certain type of praise. We can praise our pupils as much as we want for the "growth-oriented process – what they accomplished through practice, study, persistence, and [the use of] good strategies". But we should avoid the kind of praise that judges their intelligence or talent, and we should avoid the kind of praise that implies "we're proud of them for their intelligence or talent rather than for the work they put in".

Chapter Six

Managing your time

Developing presence, creating a positive learning environment and managing the classroom all takes time and effort. You need to be careful, as I cautioned in the introduction, to ensure that you don't overdo it and allow your personal life and health to suffer.

Everyone has a different way of working but being organised is clearly at the heart of it – in other words, working SMARTER not HARDER.

There are various ways to organise your workload. Here are four examples to get you started:

1. Keep lists

Prioritise tasks according to their importance and timescale; make informed decisions about the relative impact of the actions that are asked of you upon pupils' learning and well-being. For example, use a 1 to 3 scale (or traffic lights) whereby 1 is urgent (usually to be completed within 24 hours), 2 is important (within 2 to 3 days) and 3 is neutral (ideally by the end of the week but often by the end of the month or half-term). There might be a fourth category: items to be passed to someone else.

2. Delegate

Knowing which tasks can be passed to someone else and to whom is important; keeping track of those tasks – striking the right balance between giving colleagues genuine ownership of the task and ensuring it is completed on time – is also important.

3. Keep meetings short and productive

I accept that, as a new teacher, it is unlikely you'll be called upon to chair many meetings but it is possible and you will certainly be required to lead some meetings with your mentor, teaching assistant, and pupils and their parents. So here is some advice on how to make the most of meetings…

Meetings can be kept short and productive by circulating a clear, agreed agenda prior to the meeting and doggedly sticking to that agenda, ensuring that deviations are avoided.

The minutes of meetings should be short, too, and should list the actions required and the people responsible for their completion.

Meetings are often important, unavoidable and the most effective way of making decisions. But knowing when a meeting is necessary and when meetings can be avoided is just as important. Ask yourself: can I achieve the same outcome without a meeting? Can the matter be resolved by email, a telephone call or a 'walk and talk'? If a meeting is necessary, for example with a parent, pupil or external agency, what is the best format? A formal, round the table meeting or a short, standing briefing? People will respond better to meetings if they know they are only held when necessary.

4. Start a diary

Start a diary of your activities at school and at home, listing everything you do and how much time you spend on each thing. Include every activity, even those that you may not think of as big tasks: phone calls, photocopying, impromptu meetings with colleagues, etc.

You may find it useful to break your work down by structured (teaching time and scheduled non-teaching activities, PPA time, meetings, parent consultations, training) and unstructured work time.

Look back at the diary and ask yourself what patterns you might be able to change. Set yourself specific goals, making sure to write your goals up in a positive way. Goals become easier to accomplish when you focus on the benefit and not the problem. For example, set a time to finish each term night. Set free time on weekends and on some weeknights.

While you are planning, make sure that you make time for a good sleep. According to the Great British Sleep Survey, long-term poor sleepers are seven times more likely to feel helpless than good sleepers and five times more likely to feel alone. Bad sleepers are also twice as likely to have relationship problems or suffer daytime fatigue and poor concentration.

What can you do to improve your sleep? Here are a few tips:

- Don't work in your bedroom.
- Make sure you have some quiet relaxing time before bed.
- Try not to read late at night on a backlit device.

To ensure an effective balance in life, teachers need to be expert planners. The best tips to making this happen revolve around the art of real and effective time-management.

In order to achieve this, you could buy a year 'page a day' planner and produce your own A4 week plan, broken into the hours of the day. First, put in your working day commitments for the year, and then personal commitments for the year, into both the planner and your week plan. Use separate colours for different types of commitments at work, and plan in when you will do marking, and so on, during evening slots and weekends. However, ensure that you put into your weekly plan the time slots when you are going to watch your favourite television programmes, prepare and eat meals, go to the gym etc. These are vital aspects of effective time-management – you are ensuring that your personal life and wellbeing are given equal priority in your weekly plans.

Now look back at your workload. Check that the week isn't dominated by one colour on the plan. Be realistic, but also hard-nosed about this. Move work onto next week's plan or even later if it can be.

Put a copy of your plan up at work and at home. Hold yourself to account and encourage others to also hold you to account.

Say "no". When something is thrown at you at work that adds to your workload, look at your plan. Have you a slot free when it can be done this week? If not, say so. Offer to fit it into a coming week, but don't take on what you can't do.

And finally…

Ask for help when you need it

No matter what you're going through, there is help out there for you. For example, the Teacher Support Partnership is always at the end of the telephone, day or night, all the time.

Whatever you need, they are there 24/7. Their trained counsellors will listen to you without judgment and will help you think through the problems you are facing to find a way forwards and feel better. No issue is too big or too small for them.

They are available UK-wide on 08000 562 561 and via text on 07909 341229. Their helpline is free and available to all teachers and staff in education (primary, secondary, further or higher education) in England, Wales and Scotland. All calls are free of charge.

Depending on your needs they might:
- deal with your call personally and offer emotional support straight away
- offer action plan support (coaching)
- transfer you to one of their BACP-accredited counsellors for counselling
- connect you to one of their other services such as grants or information
- assist with referral for long term treatment (for example, to a doctor)

Part Three

Making Sense of the System

Chapter Seven

Schools, phases, and stages

Types of schools

All children in England between the ages of 5 and 16 are entitled to a free place at a state school. Most state schools have to follow the national curriculum.

The most common types of school are as follows:

- *community schools*, controlled by the local council and not influenced by business or religious groups
- *foundation schools*, which have more freedom to change the way they do things than community schools
- *academies*, run by a governing body, independent of the local council - they can follow a different curriculum if they wish although most do not
- *grammar schools*, run by the council, a foundation body or a trust - they select all or most of their pupils based on academic ability and there is often an exam to get in
- *special schools*, where pupils aged 11 and older with special educational needs and/or disabilities (SEND) can specialise in 1 of the 4 areas of special educational needs: communication and interaction; cognition and learning; social, emotional and mental health; and sensory and physical needs. Schools can further specialise within these categories to reflect the special needs they help with, e.g. Autistic spectrum disorders, visual impairment or speech, language and communication needs (SLCN).

Let's look at the main types of school in more detail...

Faith schools

Faith schools can be different kinds of schools, e.g. voluntary aided schools, free schools, academies etc., but are associated with a particular religion. Faith schools are mostly run like other state schools. They have to follow the national curriculum. The admissions criteria and staffing policies may be different, although anyone can apply for a place.

Free schools

Free schools are funded by the government but aren't run by the local council. They have more control over how they do things. They're 'all-ability' schools, so can't use academic selection processes like a grammar school. Free schools can set their own pay and conditions for staff, and change the length of school terms and the school day. They don't have to follow the national curriculum.

Free schools are run on a not-for-profit basis and can be set up by groups like: charities; universities; independent schools; community and faith groups; teachers; parents; and businesses. There are several types of free school including:

- *University technical colleges* – UTCs specialise in subjects like engineering and construction - and teach these subjects along with business skills and IT. Pupils study academic subjects as well as practical subjects leading to technical qualifications. The curriculum is designed by the university and employers, who also provide work experience for pupils. University technical colleges are sponsored by: universities; employers; and further education colleges.

- *Studio schools* – these are small schools (usually with around 300 pupils) delivering mainstream qualifications through project-based learning. This means working in realistic situations as well as learning academic subjects. Pupils work with local employers and a personal coach, and follow a curriculum designed to give them the skills and qualifications they need in work, or to take up further education.

Academies

Academies are publicly funded independent schools. Academies don't have to follow the national curriculum and can set their own term times. They still have to follow the same rules on admissions, special educational needs and exclusions as other state schools.

Academies get money direct from the government, not the local council. They're run by an academy trust which employs the staff. Some academies have sponsors such as businesses, universities, other schools, faith groups or voluntary groups. Sponsors are responsible for improving the performance of their schools.

City technology colleges

City technology colleges (as distinct from UTCs) are independent schools in urban areas that are free for pupils to attend. They're owned and funded by companies as well as central government (not the local council). Their curriculum places a particular emphasis on technological and practical skills.

State boarding schools

State boarding schools provide free education but charge fees for boarding. Some state boarding schools are run by local councils, and some are run as academies or free schools.

State boarding schools give priority to children who have a particular need to board and will assess children's suitability for boarding.

Private schools

Private schools (also known as 'independent schools' and, confusingly, 'public schools') charge fees to attend instead of being funded by the government, although they enjoy charitable status and therefore get tax breaks. Pupils don't have to follow the national curriculum.

All private schools must be registered with the government and are inspected regularly. All school reports are published online by the organisation responsible for inspecting them. Half of all independent schools are inspected by Ofsted. The Independent Schools Inspectorate inspects schools that are members of the Independent Schools Council. Some other schools are inspected by the School Inspection Service. There are also private schools which specialise in teaching children with special educational needs.

Phases and key stages

The education system in England is divided into four main phases:
1.   Primary education,
2.   Secondary education,
3.   Further education, and
4.   Higher education.

The education system is further split into key stages which breaks down as follows:
* Key Stage 1: 5 to 7 years old
* Key Stage 2: 7 to 11 years old
* Key Stage 3: 11 to 14 years old
* Key Stage 4: 14 to 16 years old

Primary Education

Primary education begins at the age of 5 and continues until the age of 11. It comprises the Early Years Foundation Stage (EYFS) and key stages one (KS1) and two (KS2).

Secondary Education

From the ages of 11 to 16, pupils attend secondary school for key stages three (KS3) and four (KS4) as they progress towards General Certificates in Secondary Education (GCSEs).

Further Education

Once a pupil finishes secondary education they have the option to extend into further education in order to take their Advanced Level certificates (A Levels), General National Vocational Qualifications (GNVQs), BTECs (named after the original awarding body, the Business and Technology Education Council, but now awarded by Pearson Edexcel) or other such qualifications. Alternatively, they can enter the world of work whilst continuing to study. Pupils planning to go to university must complete further education, traditionally completing A Levels.

Higher Education

Once a pupil finishes further education – usually in the form of A Levels – they can pursue their studies at university by studying towards a bachelor level degree qualification (for example, a Bachelor of Arts - or BA - or Bachelor of Science - known as a BSc).

Raising the age of participation

Children have to legally attend primary and secondary education from about 5 years old until the pupil is 16 years old. The government recently increased the age to which all young people in England are required to continue in education or training. They introduced this change in 2 stages:

1. Pupils who left Year 11 in the summer of 2013 had to continue in education or training for at least another year until June 2014

2. Pupils who left Year 11 in the summer of 2014 or later had to continue until at least their 18th birthday.

At the time of publication, therefore, the legal age of participation is 18. However, this does not mean that young people must stay in school until they reach that age. Rather, they can choose from the following options:

- Full-time education (e.g. at a school or college)
- An apprenticeship or traineeship
- Part-time education or training combined with one of the following:
  - Employment or self-employment for 20 hours or more a week
  - Volunteering for 20 hours or more a week

M J Bromley

Chapter Eight

Curriculum and qualifications

The national curriculum

The national curriculum sets out the programmes of study and attainment targets for all subjects at all four key stages. All local-authority-maintained schools in England must teach these programmes of study. The majority of the current national curriculum was introduced in September 2014. The exceptions are English, mathematics and science. English and mathematics came into force for pupils in Years 2, 6 and 10 in September 2015, and applied to pupils in Year 11 from September 2016. The science curriculum came into force for Year 10 pupils in September 2016, and for Year 11 pupils in September 2017.

Every state-funded school must offer a curriculum which is balanced and broadly based and which:
- promotes the spiritual, moral, cultural, mental and physical development of pupils at the school and of society
- prepares pupils at the school for the opportunities, responsibilities and experiences of later life

Academies are also required to offer a broad and balanced curriculum.

The school curriculum comprises all learning and other experiences that each school plans for its pupils. The national curriculum forms one part of the school curriculum.

All state schools are also required to make provision for a daily act of collective worship and must teach religious education to pupils at every key stage and sex and relationship education to pupils in secondary school.

Maintained schools in England are legally required to follow the statutory national curriculum which sets out - in the form of programmes of study and on the basis of key stages - the subject content for those subjects that should be taught to all pupils. All schools must publish their school curriculum by subject and academic year online.

All schools must make provision for personal, social, health and economic education (PSHE), drawing on good practice. Schools are also free to include other subjects or topics of their choice in planning and designing their own programme of education.

The aims of the national curriculum

The national curriculum aims to provide pupils with an introduction to the essential knowledge they need to be educated citizens. It introduces pupils to "the best that has been thought and said" (as Matthew Arnold put it), and helps engender an appreciation of human creativity and achievement.

The national curriculum is just one element in the education of every child. There should be time and space in the school day and in each week, term and year to range beyond the national curriculum specifications.

The national curriculum provides an outline of core knowledge around which teachers can develop exciting and stimulating lessons to promote the development of pupils' knowledge, understanding and skills as part of the wider school curriculum.

The structure of the national curriculum

The national curriculum is organised on the basis of four key stages and 12 subjects, classified in legal terms as 'core' and 'other foundation' subjects. The structure of the national curriculum, in terms of which subjects are compulsory at each key stage, is as follows...

The core subjects are English, mathematics and science and all of them are compulsory from key stage 1 to key stage 4 inclusive.

The foundation subjects are art and design which is compulsory from key stage 1 to 3, citizenship which is compulsory in key stages 1 and 2, computing (key stage 1 to 4), design and technology (KS1-3), languages (KS2 and 3), geography (KS1-3), history (KS1-

3), music (KS1-3), and physical education (KS1-4).

All schools are also required to teach religious education at all key stages. In addition, secondary schools must provide sex and relationship education.

Key stage 4 entitlement areas

The arts (comprising art and design, music, dance, drama and media arts), design and technology, the humanities (comprising geography and history) and modern foreign languages are not compulsory national curriculum subjects after the age of 14, but all pupils in maintained schools have a statutory entitlement to be able to study a subject in each of those 4 areas.

Let's take a look at some key aspects of the curriculum...

Numeracy and mathematics

Teachers should use every relevant subject to develop pupils' mathematical fluency. Confidence in numeracy and other mathematical skills is a precondition of success across the national curriculum. Teachers should develop pupils' numeracy and mathematical reasoning in all subjects so that they understand and appreciate the importance of mathematics. Pupils should be taught to apply arithmetic fluently to problems, understand and use measures, make estimates and sense-check their work. Pupils should apply their geometric and algebraic understanding, and relate their understanding of probability to the notions of risk and uncertainty. They should also understand the cycle of collecting, presenting and analysing data. They should be taught to apply their mathematics to both routine and non-routine problems, including breaking down more complex problems into a series of simpler steps.

Language and literacy

Teachers should develop pupils' spoken language, reading, writing and vocabulary as integral aspects of the teaching of every subject. English is both a subject in its own right and the medium for teaching; for pupils, understanding the language provides access to the whole curriculum. Fluency in the English language is an essential foundation for success in all subjects.

Spoken language

Pupils should be taught to speak clearly and convey ideas confidently using Standard English. They should learn to justify ideas with reasons; ask questions to check understanding; develop vocabulary and build knowledge; negotiate; evaluate and build on the ideas of others; and select the appropriate register for effective communication. They should be taught to give well-structured descriptions and explanations and develop their understanding through speculating, hypothesising and exploring ideas. This will enable them to clarify their thinking as well as organise their ideas for writing.

Reading and writing

Teachers should develop pupils' reading and writing in all subjects to support their acquisition of knowledge. Pupils should be taught to read fluently, understand extended prose (both fiction and non-fiction) and be encouraged to read for pleasure. Schools should do everything to promote wider reading. They should provide library facilities and set ambitious expectations for reading at home. Pupils should develop the stamina and skills to write at length, with accurate spelling and punctuation. They should be taught the correct use of grammar. They should build on what they have been taught in order to expand the range of their writing and the variety of the grammar they use. The writing they do should include narratives, explanations, descriptions, comparisons, summaries and evaluations. Such writing supports them in rehearsing, understanding and consolidating what they have heard or read.

Vocabulary development

Pupils' acquisition and command of vocabulary are key to their learning and progress across the whole curriculum. Teachers should therefore develop vocabulary actively, building systematically on pupils' current knowledge. They should increase pupils' store of words in general. Simultaneously, they should also make links between known and new vocabulary and discuss the shades of meaning in similar words. In this way, pupils expand the vocabulary choices that are available to them when they write. In addition, it is vital for pupils' comprehension that they understand the meanings of words they meet in their reading across all subjects, and older pupils should be taught the meaning of instruction verbs that they may meet in examination questions. It is particularly important to induct pupils into the language which defines each subject in its own right, such as accurate mathematical and scientific language.

Statutory assessment

As part of the recent reforms to the national curriculum, the previous system of national curriculum 'levels' which were used up to the end of key stage 3 to report children's attainment and progress have been removed and not replaced. By removing levels, the government hoped to allow teachers greater flexibility in the way that they planned and assessed pupils' learning.

The programmes of study within the new curriculum set out expectations at the end of each key stage, and all schools were free to develop a curriculum relevant to their pupils that teaches this content. The curriculum must include an assessment system which enables schools to check what pupils have learned and whether they are on track to meet expectations at the end of the key stage, and to report regularly to parents.

There are national curriculum tests and teacher assessments at the end of key stages 1 and 2. New key stage 1 and key stage 2 tests in English, mathematics and science, based on the new curriculum, were introduced in the summer of 2016.

From 2015-16, KS2 test outcomes have been reported as a scaled score, where the expected score is 100 and pupil progress is determined in relation to the average progress made by pupils with the same baseline (i.e. the same KS1 average point score). For example, if a pupil has an APS of 19 at KS1, the government calculates the average scaled score in the KS2 tests for all pupils with an APS of 19 in order to see whether the pupil in question achieved a higher or lower scaled score than that average

There are no longer statutory tests at the end of key stage 3 although many schools continue to use some form of end of key stage assessment in order to report this data to parents.

Statutory tests

Early Years Foundation Stage (EYFS)

Teachers complete a profile at the end of EYFS using the following rating:

1 = Indicates a pupil who is at the 'emerging' level at the end of the EYFS;

2 = Indicates a pupil who is at the 'expected' level at the end of the EYFS;

3 = Indicates a pupil who is at the 'exceeding' level at the end of the EYFS;

A = Indicates a pupil who has not been assessed due to long periods of absence, for instance a prolonged illness.

Key stage 1

Since 2016 KS1 national curriculum test outcomes have been reported using scaled scores. At this time, a new set of KS1 national curriculum tests replaced the previous tests and tasks.

The new tests consist of:

- English reading Paper 1
- English reading Paper 2
- Mathematics Paper 1: arithmetic
- Mathematics Paper 2: reasoning
- English grammar, punctuation and spelling papers are also sent to schools but there is no legal requirement to administer them or to use the result to inform teacher assessment. There is no test for English writing. Instead, this is achieved through teacher assessment.

National curriculum tests are designed to be as similar as possible year on year, but slight differences in difficulty will occur between years. Scaled scores maintain their meaning over time so that two pupils achieving the same scaled score in different years will have demonstrated the same attainment. For the KS1 tests a scaled score of 100 will always represent the 'expected standard'. A pupil's scaled score will be based on their raw score. The raw score is the total number of marks a pupil receives in a test, based on the number of questions they answered correctly. The pupil's raw score will be translated into a scaled score using a conversion table.

Key stage 2

From 2016 KS2 national curriculum test outcomes have also been reported using scaled scores. There is only one set of tests for each subject. The tests include a small number of questions designed to assess the most able pupils. The KS2 tests consist of:

- English reading
- English grammar, punctuation and spelling Paper 1: short answer questions
- English grammar, punctuation and spelling Paper 2: spelling
- Mathematics Paper 1: arithmetic
- Mathematics Paper 2: reasoning
- Mathematics Paper 3: reasoning

Since 2016 schools have been held to account for the percentage of pupils achieving the expected standard at the end of KS2 and whether they made sufficient progress based on a new value added measure of progress. A school is deemed to fall below the floor standard where fewer than 65% of pupils achieve the expected standard and pupils do not make sufficient progress.

Key stage 3

There are no statutory tests in key stage 3

Key stage 4

Pupils in key stage 4 sit GCSE examinations.

The government recently reformed GCSEs. Specifically:

- the content for all subjects has been revised - in most instances by the Department for Education
- assessment is by means of a new grading scale from 9 to 1

(replacing A*-U grades)

- non-exam assessment is only used where knowledge, skills and understanding cannot be tested validly in an exam; this means the proportion of non-exam assessment has been reduced in a number of subjects
- tiering (having a separate foundation and higher exam paper) is only used when a single exam cannot assess pupils across the full ability range in a way that enables them all to demonstrate their knowledge, skills and understanding; this means fewer subjects will now use tiering
- November exams are only available in Maths and English language, and only for pupils who were 16 or over on the preceding 31 August; all other exams will take place in the summer (putting an end to re-sits).

Post-16

At post-16, level 2 pupils (that is to say those who did not achieve 'good passes' in five or more GCSEs - i.e. grade C or above under the old system or grade 4 or above under the new system) are expected to do one of two things:

- Retake their GCSEs; or
- Study towards a 'substantial vocational qualification' which provides the knowledge and skills necessary to enter a trade or skilled occupation, whilst also retaking their English and/or mathematics GCSEs if they did not achieve a 'good pass' in either or both of these subjects.

At Level 3, meanwhile, pupils will have the option of studying one of three pathways:

- Academic A Levels;
- Tech Levels; or
- Applied General Qualifications.

All three types of qualification at level 3 can provide a route into higher education because they all carry UCAS (which stands for the University and Colleges Admissions Service) points. From 2016, Tech Levels and Applied General Qualifications (or AGQs) are the only vocational qualifications to be included in the 16-19 league tables. Of course, other approved vocational qualifications can still be offered but they will not be included in league tables.

Academic A Levels

A levels are now fully linear with end-of-course assessments covering knowledge and understanding across the whole course; course content was recently revised, except in Maths, so that a greater proportion of exam questions require extended answers and there are fewer short-answer questions.

AS Levels

Although AS Levels (the first year of two-year post-16 studies) continue to be taught, they are no longer regarded as stand-alone 'stepping-stones' to A-Levels. Instead, AS Levels are a one-year course whose content is the same as the first year of A Levels.

Chapter Nine

Accountability and inspection

What is accountability?

The term 'accountability' refers to a minimum expectation or standard regarding the effectiveness of a particular activity. The rationale for being accountability as teachers resides in the fact that state education is a publicly-funded and universal state service. Education is therefore in the public interest and so the education system must be accountable both at the national and local level.

The accountability system in English education is formed of a combination of hierarchical and market accountability.

Hierarchical accountability

Schools are held accountable through hierarchical structures for a variety of aspects of their performance. For example, schools and their governing bodies are accountable to their local authority or the Department for Education, and to Ofsted for their national test and examination results.

Schools are also accountable to local authorities and the Department for Education for how they spend resources and can be challenged by auditors within the local authority.

The sanctions which can be applied within a system of hierarchical accountability take a number of forms. A negative Ofsted inspection can have serious consequences for the viability of a school. The Secretary of State for Education can direct a local authority to consider a warning notice, when the standards of a school are deemed to be unacceptably low. Once a warning notice has been issued the Secretary of State is also able to appoint additional governors or replace a governing body with an interim executive board. Further reputational sanctions, such as publicly 'naming and shaming' schools and replacing head teachers and senior leaders are also associated with the hierarchical accountability regime.

Market accountability

The role of market accountability in education has been promoted by new government policies which have sought to make available a range of information by which consumers such as parents can hold English schools accountable in the market place.

Information is available to parents in a variety of forms. The first is the results of national tests taken and 11, 16 and 18. The second source of information is the reports of school inspections carried out by Ofsted. Collectively, these different sources of information impact upon a school's reputation and inform consumer choice.

The sanctions which can applied within a system of market accountability include the possibility of a parent choosing to take their child out of the school and the school closing if consumer demand declines significantly. A more likely outcome is a reduction in funding: as funding is primarily based on pupil numbers, if a school becomes less popular and the numbers decrease, its budget will decrease.

Characteristics of the English education accountability system

The three bodies to which each maintained primary and secondary school is accountable for its performance are the local authority, Ofsted and the Department for Education.

Local authorities are tasked with monitoring school performance and helping schools improve, not least by appointing School Improvement Partners (serving heads, former heads and local authority advisors) to provide assistance, advice and challenge.

Ofsted inspectors visit and observe schools before producing inspection reports containing qualitative and quantitative analysis setting out whether and where schools need to improve.

The Department for Education's judgments are based largely on quantitative measures. The Department rates school performance against a range of statistical criteria and sets this out in achievement and attainment tables.

The primary purpose of any system of administrative accountability is to measure performance as a first step towards securing improvement. This process begins within schools, and is led by head teachers and governors.

In practice, this means that teachers are accountable for ensuring:
- good levels of behaviour within their classrooms
- curriculum content is covered
- lessons are planned effectively so pupils are engaged and challenged
- pupils' work is marked in a timely way and feedback is given
- assessment information is entered into data management systems
- parental reports are written in an accurate and timely way
- professional conduct at all times, both in and out of school
- they contribute to all aspects of school life including parents' evenings and events
- the Teachers' Standards are upheld

The Department for Education – roles and responsibilities

The Department for Education is responsible for education and children's services in England. They work to achieve a highly educated society in which opportunity is equal for children and young people, no matter what their background or family circumstances. They are responsible for:
- teaching and learning for children in the early years and in primary schools
- teaching and learning for young people under the age of 19 in secondary schools and in further education
- supporting professionals who work with children and young people
- helping disadvantaged children and young people to achieve more
- making sure that local services protect and support children

Recently, a cabinet reshuffle has made the Department for Education responsible for higher education including universities.

The Department's priorities are:

- Safety and wellbeing: ensuring all children and young people are protected from harm and vulnerable children are supported to succeed with opportunities as good as those for any other child.
- Educational excellence: ensuring every child and young person can access high-quality provision, achieving to the best of his or her ability regardless of location, attainment and background.
- Preparedness for adult life: ensuring all 19-year-olds complete school or college with the skills and character to contribute to the UK's society and economy and are able to access high-quality work or study options.

The Department is a ministerial department with three executive agencies:

- Education Funding Agency (EFA)
- Standards and Testing Agency (STA)
- National College for Teaching and Leadership (NCTL)

As a result of the reshuffle, the Standards Funding Agency (SFA) now also falls within the Department's purview.

Ofsted – roles and responsibilities

Ofsted is the Office for Standards in Education, Children's Services and Skills. They inspect and regulate services that care for children and young people, and services providing education and skills for learners of all ages. Every week, they carry out hundreds of inspections and regulatory visits throughout England and publish the results online. They help providers that are not yet of good standard to improve, monitor their progress and share with them the best practice they find. They report directly to Parliament and are independent and impartial. They have around 1,500 employees across eight regions. They also directly contract with more than 1,500 so-called 'Ofsted Inspectors', many of whom are active school and college leaders, to carry out inspections of schools and further education and skills provision. Ofsted is a member of the National Preventative Mechanism, which monitors and reports on places of detention such as prisons.

Ofsted are responsible for:

- inspecting maintained schools and academies, some independent schools, and many other educational institutions and programmes outside of higher education
- inspecting childcare, adoption and fostering agencies and initial teacher training
- publishing reports of their findings so they can be used to improve the overall quality of education and training
- regulating a range of early years and children's social care services, making sure they're suitable for children and potentially vulnerable young people
- reporting to policymakers on the effectiveness of these services

Regional schools commissioners

Schools commissioners work with school leaders to take action in underperforming academy schools.

Regional schools commissioners (RSCs) act on behalf of the Secretary of State for Education, largely in place of the local authority, and are accountable to the National Schools Commissioner.

Each RSC is supported by a head teacher board (HTB). HTBs are made up of experienced academy head teachers and other sector leaders who advise and challenge RSCs on the decisions they make. RSCs also work closely with a number of partners.

RSCs' main responsibilities include:

- taking action where academies and free schools are underperforming
- intervening in academies where governance is inadequate
- deciding on applications from local-authority-maintained schools to convert to academy status
- improving underperforming maintained schools by providing

them with support from a strong sponsor
- encouraging and deciding on applications from sponsors to operate in a region
- taking action to improve poorly performing sponsors
- advising on proposals for new free schools
- advising on whether to cancel, defer or enter into funding agreements with free school projects
- deciding on applications to make significant changes to academies and free schools

Head teacher boards

Head teacher boards (HTBs) are responsible for advising their RSC, contributing their local knowledge and professional expertise to help the RSC's decision-making. This can involve assessing school performance data, reviewing the governance structure of a new multi-academy trust or challenging a school's improvement plan. In some cases, HTB members also carry out additional duties for RSCs in their regions.

RSCs and HTBs also make use of local networks to gather information to support their decisions.

Each HTB is made up of 4 to 8 members. HTB members are generally head teachers, former head teachers, trustees or business leaders. Local academy head teachers elect 4 members on each HTB. Each HTB member, no matter how they are appointed, has equal status.

School governors

The key responsibilities of a governing body include:
- ensuring the quality of educational provision;
- challenging and monitoring the performance of the school;
- ensuring good financial health and probity;
- supporting the school leadership team with the management of staff.

In fulfilling these responsibilities an effective governing body:
- helps the school to set high standards by planning for the

school's future and setting targets for school improvement;
- keeps the pressure up on school improvement;
- acts as a critical friend to the school, offering support and advice;
- helps the school respond to the needs of parents and the community;
- makes the school accountable to the public for what it does;
- works with the school on planning, developing policies and keeping these under review;
- exercises its responsibilities and powers in partnership with the head teacher and staff; and
- does not intervene in the day-to-day management of the school unless there are weaknesses in the school, when it then has a duty to take action.

Governors of academy schools are also charity trustees. There are three core duties with which charity trustees must comply. These are:
1. The duty of compliance,
2. The duty of prudence, and
3. The duty of care.

Local authorities

Many parts of England have two tiers of local government:
- county councils
- district, borough or city councils

In some parts of the country, however, there is just one (unitary) tier of local government providing all the local services.

County councils

These are responsible for services across the whole of a county, like:
- education
- transport
- planning
- fire and public safety

- social care
- libraries
- waste management
- trading standards

District, borough and city councils

These cover a smaller area than county councils. They're usually responsible for services like:
- rubbish collection
- recycling
- Council Tax collections
- housing
- planning applications

Local authorities are gradually losing responsibility for schools as schools elect to convert to academy status and thus become accountable to central, rather than local, government. However, local authorities retain responsibilities for allocating school places.

Part Four

Managing Your Classroom

Chapter Ten

Strategies for classroom management

Part Four of this book is all about classroom management - how to ensure pupils behave well so that they can learn and make progress.

In Chapter Eleven we will take a look at some of the most common examples of misbehaviour and explore the best strategies for dealing with them. In Chapter Twelve we will consider the role of rewards and sanctions in the classroom, celebrating good behaviour but punishing poor behaviour.

But first let's take a step back and consider why pupils might not always do and say what we want them to...

Broadly speaking, pupils misbehave for one of four reasons:
- They are bored.
- They are stuck.
- They have additional and different needs.
- They are naughty.

When pupils are bored, they might entertain themselves by being naughty. They might talk, throw paper darts, they might stick pencils up their nostrils and sing hallelujah. They are either trying to alleviate their boredom or trying to make you aware that they're bored and need more challenge, or indeed both.

When they are stuck, they might send up metaphorical smoke signals by being naughty in order to draw your attention to their difficulty. Alternatively, they might try to mask the fact they're stuck by being naughty. Either way it's a cry for help.

Whether they're bored or stuck, the cure for their behaviour is better differentiation, because clearly the work isn't appropriately pitched. If they are bored, the work is too easy. If they are stuck, the work is too hard. What you want is to pitch the work in the so-called 'struggle zone' - hard but achievable. In other words, the work you set must be difficult enough to provide challenge, but not so difficult as to be impossible.

Pupils with additional and different needs such as pupils with ADHD cannot always control the way they behave. They may lack social skills or have difficulty concentrating. Whatever the circumstances, you are not alone in dealing with pupils who have emotional and behavioural difficulties, should seek expert help, and follow your school's policies at all times.

But sometimes pupils are neither bored nor stuck, and do not have any specific learning needs or disabilities: they are just plain old-fashioned naughty. Perhaps it's fun, a distraction, a means of reminding others of their existence. Of course, you need to be careful here because sometimes pupils with EBD/SEND can present as being 'naughty'. In every case, you should seek help and advice from your SENCO and other experienced colleagues and always consult your pupil data. As I say above, you are not alone and you should always follow your school's policies at all times. Your school may have a 'three strikes and you're out' rule, for example, which gives you a framework to work within which pupils cannot argue with or try to negotiate with.

Whatever the motivation, it is not an indictment of the way the teacher is teaching. So you are not to blame for pupils' misbehaviour and you are not responsible for it either. But, as the adult in the room with a responsibility for teaching, you do have a role to play creating a climate which minimises misbehaviour as well as a duty to respond to misbehaviour when it happens.

So let's now turn our attentions to some classroom management strategies that you can use when pupils are naughty for naughty's sake.

Top 10 tips for managing your classroom

1. Demonstrate your authority by the position you take in the room; keep on your feet as much as possible and be where you can watch everything that is going on. Pupils should believe that you have eyes in the back of your head.

2. Establish a set of rules which make desired behaviours explicit and display them prominently in the room, referring to them as often as possible so that they don't disappear.

3. Reward the right behaviours more than you sanction the wrong ones. The goal is to establish the habit of co-operation.

4. Get a pupil's full attention before giving instructions. Be very clear in all your instructions and expectations.

5. A pupil's behaviour is reinforced when s/he gets attention for it, but don't be tempted simply to ignore it. Find a calm and quiet way to let the pupil know that you see exactly what s/he is doing and that there is a consequence, without making a fuss, getting upset or sounding annoyed.

6. Avoid confrontational situations where you or the pupil has to publicly back down. Talk to the pupil in terms of her/his choices and the consequences of those choices, and then give sufficient "take-up" time.

7. Never attempt to start teaching a lesson until the pupils are ready.

8. Do not teach up to the last minute and rush because the next class is waiting. Allow time to answer questions, review that day's learning, outline plans for the next lesson, and put equipment away.

9. Use positive language. For example, instead of "will you stop talking", say "I'd like everyone listening"; instead of "stop turning around", say "I'd like everyone facing this way please".

10. Use positive body language. Gain their attention with eye contact before you say what you want to say.

Seven strategies for behaviour management

Let's now explore in greater depth seven proven strategies for managing behaviour, namely:

1.   Lead by example
2.   Stay positive
3.   Every day is a clean slate
4.   Ensure all the adults work together
5.   Reward good behaviour
6.   Divert poor behaviour
7.   Sanctions are a last resort

Lead by example

At the start of the lesson, stand at the door smiling: show the class you are enthusiastic about teaching them and that your classroom is a happy, friendly place to learn. Greet each pupil with a smile and a friendly 'hello' as they enter the room. Such an approach not only shows your class that you enjoy teaching them and will treat each pupil as an individual; it also models the way you expect your pupils to behave.

Stay positive

Try your best to stay positive throughout the lesson: try to avoid using negative words or body language, and remember you're not there to judge pupils; you're there to help them learn. When you need to discipline a pupil, ensure you distinguish between their behaviour and them as a person – it is the behaviour that was inappropriate not the pupil. By staying positive, you are once again modelling the types of behaviours you expect from pupils – you are showing them you expect them, too, to stay in control of their emotions. Try to remain polite at all times: say 'please' and 'thank you' to pupils and make sure every pupil (even the quiet ones) is acknowledged for his or her contributions to the lesson.

Every day is a clean slate

Ensure that incidents are dealt with and, where possible, resolved by the end of the day on which they take place. The next day should be a fresh start for everyone: make clear through your choice of words and body language that those pupils who misbehaved yesterday are starting today with a clean slate. Begin the day with high expectations of every pupil – each new day is a new start.

Ensure all the adults work together

If you have another adult working with you in the classroom, such as a teaching assistant, make sure you have agreed with them in advance how you will tackle behaviour matters. You need to ensure you both speak with one voice and are certain the other will support and mirror your actions and decisions. It is no good for you or for your pupils if the adults in the room have different ways of approaching behaviour management and are seen to disagree about how to discipline pupils. Not only will this send mixed signals to pupils; it will also pave the way for pupils to argue with you and try to drive a wedge between you and the other adult.

Reward good behaviour

The best way of dealing with inappropriate behaviour is through the positive reinforcement of good behaviours. Not only does rewarding good behaviour ensure that those pupils who behave well and work hard receive recognition for their efforts; it also models for those pupils who misbehave exactly what is expected of them, too. Praise for good behaviour and good work should be sincere and appropriate to the age and ability of the pupil.

Divert poor behaviour

If poor behaviour becomes disruptive to the learning, try to divert it in an unobtrusive manner. Use eye contact or questions to distract pupils who are misbehaving and make them aware you have noticed their misbehaviour and now want them to refocus on the lesson. If poor behaviour continues, try to find a way to prevent it such as changing your seating plan or altering the way in which your classroom is set up before punishing the pupil.

If necessary, talk to the pupil about their behaviour and make clear that their behaviour falls below the standard you expect of them – and, crucially, that their behaviour falls below the standard you know they are capable of producing. Ask them why they have not been able to stay focused on the lesson, ask them to find ways of avoiding a repeat of it in the future.

Most of the time, pupils are harsher critics of their own behaviour than we are as teachers. Pupils will often provide sensible solutions such as asking to move seats or requesting work which is more appropriate to their ability. In such cases, make sure the conversation is private – do not make an example of pupils by publicly disciplining them in front of the class. Take them to one side, perhaps outside the classroom, and talk to them calmly and quietly, allowing them the time and opportunity to explain.

Notwithstanding this, you still need to be firm and need to make sure that the pupil understands they have been warned; make sure they know the consequences of any further disruption.

Sanctions are a last resort

Try to avoid sanctions wherever possible: they only punish poor behaviour; they do not prevent poor behaviour being repeated, nor do they help the pupil to learn from their mistakes. When sanctions are appropriate, make sure the pupil has been afforded the time and opportunity to rectify their mistakes and to make choices about their future behaviour. Try to catch them doing the right thing and give them positive feedback for it. When you apply the sanction, do so with empathy and patience, show you care about the pupil and are disappointed you have been left no option but to punish them. Make clear you are punishing the pupil's behaviour and not the pupil; you are not labelling them or judging them.

Chapter Eleven

Dealing with common misbehaviours

Misbehaviour in the classroom usually presents itself in one of five ways:
1.	Defiance
2.	Disruption
3.	Disturbing behaviour
4.	Discourtesy
5.	Distraction

Here's how best to respond to each of these five misbehaviours…

1. Defiant behaviour

If a pupil talks back or laughs at the teacher, claims the teacher is unfair or blames others for their misbehaviour, consider the underlying causes of this type of defiance. Perhaps the pupil has low self-esteem or does not get much attention at home and at school. Perhaps the pupil is trying to assert some kind of control because he or she feels powerless to make decisions in his or her life. The best way to deal with this type of behaviour, it would follow, is to:

Be detached: do not take it personally; it is not aimed at you. Avoid escalating the situation into a power struggle. Model a considered, mature and adult response. Avoid raising your voice or giving ultimatums which only serve to antagonise the pupil further and achieve nothing.

Take time out: pause, allow time for the situation to cool, allow time for the pupil to retract their statement or reconsider what they are trying to say.

Remove the audience: suggest you talk about it later so that the pupil can tell you what concerns them rather than conducting a public argument in front of the class.

Be respectful: show you care about the pupil and will respect them

– tell them you expect the pupil to extend the same courtesy to you.

Let them do some good: don't sulk, allow the pupil the opportunity to do something well, to achieve something tangible, perhaps give them a class responsibility. If they do something well, reward them with a sincere 'thank you' and 'well done'. This not only helps to defuse the situation and proves you value them; it helps raise their self-esteem.

As I say above, you are not alone, you should seek help and always follow your school's policies at all times.

2. Disruptive behaviour

If a pupil makes silly noises in the classroom or purposefully tries to annoy the teacher, consider why he or she is doing this: perhaps the pupil is bored or struggling with the work you have set but doesn't want to admit they are finding it difficult. Perhaps the pupil is seeking attention because they do not get it at home or have low self-esteem. Or perhaps they have high self-esteem and want to be the class clown, entertaining others. Then deal with it as follows:

Proactive planning: if a pupil is persistently disruptive, it is likely the result of boredom or fear of failure – you can therefore avoid it through careful planning. Better planning will ensure the work you set is more engaging and accessible and will help prevent persistently disruptive behaviour. Think about your seating plan, too. If you decide to move a pupil, make the pupil see you are doing it to help them not to punish them.

Teach empathy: show the pupil how they're affecting others' learning, encourage the pupil to see the effect they're having on other pupils. Show the pupil that their behaviour is not gaining them positive attention but is liable to lose them friends if it persists.

Reward their good behaviour: stay attentive to them at other times and try to catch them doing something good! Praise them whenever possible to reinforce the positive behaviours you expect and to give them the attention they seek in a more positive context. They want attention so give it to them when they are not misbehaving rather than when they are. If the pupil is playing the role of the class clown, try to see the funny side – laugh along with them and show them you have a sense of humour – but also teach them that sometimes it is inappropriate to be the clown. They need to know when it is and is not acceptable.

Distract their behaviour: as above, try to deal with the behaviour in an unobtrusive way by diverting them with eye contact or a question, or by involving them in the lesson more.

3. Disturbing behaviour

If a pupil uses abusive language or is loud and confrontational towards you or other pupils, it is likely the result of attention-seeking or a lack of social skills such as self-control and anger management. It's possible it might also be a way of hiding their inability to complete the work you've set. So, the best way to deal with it is as follows:

Remain calm and quiet: remind the pupil in a measured tone – and without drawing too much attention to it – that such behaviour will not be tolerated. Calmly remind the pupil of what is expected in your classroom and explain that bad language would be equally frowned upon elsewhere, that it would not be tolerated in a place of work or a public space.

Don't give them oxygen: having calmly explained how bad language or abusive behaviour will not be tolerated, quickly move on. It's important the pupil knows such behaviour is inappropriate but it's also important that such behaviour doesn't divert the class from their learning and the pupil isn't given too much attention or they will repeat the behaviour.

Teach social skills: longer term, it might be necessary to teach social skills such as managing your emotions and showing empathy for others. Consider how you might incorporate the teaching of social and emotional skills into your lessons, perhaps the next time you do group work you might have a class discussion about the social skills needed for effective team-work.

4. Discourteous behaviour

If a pupil is disrespectful towards others – for example, a pupil might ignore the teacher, roll his or her eyes or tut and sigh – it is likely the result of frustration and unhappiness. They may have been hurt and now want to take their anger and resentment out on others. The best response to such behaviour is as follows:

Remember it's not personal: try to remind yourself that such behaviour is not aimed at you personally but is symptomatic of other issues. Therefore, try to remain calm and considered, patient and caring. Remind the pupil of the consequences should they choose to continue to behave in this way; make the pupil see that they have a choice, they are in control.

Remove the audience: as above, it is important to avoid a public confrontation which will only exacerbate the situation. Keep your cool and try to remove the conflict, perhaps by asking the pupil to follow you outside for a quiet chat. Encourage the pupil to empathise with you: tell them you don't feel you deserved to be spoken to in that way and that you only want to help them. This way, you show the pupil you care about them and are hurt by the way they spoke to you; you also show the pupil that you are not the enemy.

5. Distracting behaviour

If a pupil shouts out, makes inappropriate comments or tries to involve the teacher in irrelevant or inappropriate conversations, consider why they are behaving in this way. Is disrupting the lesson a way of getting attention? Is distracting the teacher from the task in hand a way of gaining power? Try to deal with it as follows:

Plan for group work: give the pupil opportunities to work with their peers in order to practice their social skills. Give them a class responsibility so that they can assert some power and control in a more positive context.

Don't rise to it: as above, stay calm and patient at all times and do not fight fire with fire. Instead, ensure the lesson continues to flow by diverting their behaviour with eye contact, by moving closer to them or by engaging them in a class discussion. Give the pupil plenty of opportunities to contribute to the lesson, that way they might not feel the need to contribute to it when it is inappropriate to do so.

Have a private chat: if a pupil persistently distracts the lesson – and indeed you – have a private word with them as soon as possible. Explain to them how their behaviour is affecting other pupils' learning and remind them that your job is to teach and theirs is to learn – you cannot allow anyone to get in the way of this. If the pupil says they are not aware of their inappropriate behaviour, agree on a gesture you could use when they next behave inappropriately so that they will recognise the inappropriate behaviour and try to avoid it. After the chat, try to catch them doing something right – praise them for their effort or contribution. Show them that you value them as a member of the class and that you notice them when they're working hard not just when they distract you.

Above all else, make time for these pupils: they will quickly come to respect the teacher who shows an interest in them and cares about them.

Chapter Twelve

Using rewards and sanctions

Broadly speaking, behaviour management strategies including the ones we've explored in the previous two chapters, fall into three categories:

1. **Preventative** - those strategies which prevent misbehaviour from occurring, including by being clear about what is expected of pupils and what will happen if those expectations are not met.

2. **Corrective** - those strategies which correct misbehaviour once it's occurred, including by making clear that a pupil has misbehaved and sanctioning them.

3. **Supportive** - those strategies which involve working with a pupil *after* their have misbehaved in order to identify why they misbehaved and how they can avoid doing so again.

Preventative behaviour management is about having a pupil contract or a clear set of rules which are known and understood by pupils. It is about having a clear set of rewards and sanctions to encourage good behaviour and dissuade pupils from misbehaving. But it is also about how your classroom is organised: using an appropriate seating plan, having appropriate activities which challenge and support in equal measure, having appropriate pace and variety, and having the right resources. It is also about how the curriculum and timetable are organised: making sure learning pathways are appropriate for every pupil and there is an alternative curriculum for those who cannot access or are not motivated by the traditional curriculum. Finally, preventative behaviour management is about reinforcing the rules as often as possible.

Corrective behaviour management is about you, the teacher, reinforcing what is expected of pupils in every lesson, being consistent in how you discipline pupils and fair in applying sanctions. Corrective behaviour management is also about you following up on incidents.

Supportive behaviour management is about what happens after you have corrected a pupil's behaviour. It is about exploring why a pupil misbehaved in the first place in order to avoid a repeat. It is about setting out what is expected of the pupil next and about agreeing a new contract: agreeing that, next time, the sanction will be different (the next stage up); agreeing a means of avoiding misbehaviour (e.g. a 'time out' card, a mentor, counselling, etc.).

Rewards, therefore, are preventative; sanctions are corrective. Together they are, it would follow, only two-thirds of the behaviour management process and support and follow-up are also needed.

It is tempting to think in terms of rewards AND sanctions as two separate entities. But they are not. All good teachers connect their rewards with their sanctions and vice versa. Rewards and sanctions are used in tandem, they support and complement each other.

Roughly speaking, rewards should outnumber sanctions and you should reward model behaviour because, to do so, can significantly reduce the number of sanctions needed.

Start from the premise that young people enjoy being effectively rewarded. Rewards, therefore, can motivate pupils to do well. By rewarding model behaviour – as publicly as possible – you are showing others what is expected of them, you are showing others what good behaviour looks like.

You are giving attention to good behaviour (and to those pupils who behave well and work hard) rather than to those who fall short of what is expected of them.

One final word of warning: praise can be damaging. There is mounting evidence that those who are motivated by extrinsic rewards lose interest in what they are doing because they are doing it, not for the enjoyment and interest of the thing itself, but for external rewards. In other words, if pupils are encouraged to learn simply because learning leads to rewards then their interest in what they're learning will suffer.

There is also evidence that pupils who are praised for being intelligent, rather than for their hard work, are less likely to succeed…

The psychologist Carol Dweck conducted research with hundreds of pupils, mostly early adolescents. She gave each pupil a set of ten fairly different problems to solve from a non-verbal IQ test. Most of the pupils did pretty well and when they'd finished, she praised them. She praised some of the pupils for their ability (e.g., 'You got such a high score, you must be really smart'); she praised the others for their effort (e.g., 'You got such a high score, you must have worked really hard'). Both groups were exactly equal to begin with. But after receiving praise, they began to differ. The pupils whose ability was praised were pushed into the fixed mindset. When they were given a choice, they rejected a challenging new task that they could learn from, favouring more of the same instead. Why? Because they didn't want to do anything which would expose flaws in their intelligence and bring their talent into question. In contrast, 90% of the pupils whose effort was praised wanted to try the challenging new task precisely because they could learn from it.

All the pupils were given new challenging tasks to do. None of the pupils did particularly well. Those who were praised for their ability now thought they weren't very smart after all because, if success means they are intelligent, then failure must mean they're deficient. Those praised for effort, on the other hand, didn't see it as failure. They believed it meant they had to try harder. As for the pupils' enjoyment of the task, all pupils enjoyed the first task but those praised for ability did not enjoy the harder task because it isn't fun when your talent is called into question. Those praised for effort, however, said they still enjoyed it and indeed some felt the harder task was more fun because they had to exert more effort in order to try complete it.

As the tests were IQ tests, Dweck concluded that praising ability actually lowered pupils' IQs whereas praising effort raised them. Dweck also states that praising children's intelligence harms their motivation and harms their performance. Why? Because although children love to be praised, especially for their talents, as soon as they hit a snag their confidence goes out of the window and their motivation hits rock bottom. If success means they're smart, then failure means they're dumb.

Dweck talks about hidden messages in the praise we give our children. The statement, 'You learned that so quickly, you must be really smart' can be translated in a child's mind to: 'If I don't learn something quickly, I'm not smart'. Similarly, the statement 'You're so brilliant, you got an A without even trying' can be translated in a child's mind to: 'I'd better quit whilst I'm ahead or they won't think I'm smart anymore'.

This doesn't mean we shouldn't praise children, Dweck argues. But it does mean we should only use a certain type of praise. We can praise our pupils as much as we want for the "growth-oriented process - what they accomplished through practice, study, persistence, and good strategies". But we should avoid the kind of praise that judges their intelligence or talent, and we should avoid the kind of praise that implies we're proud of them for their intelligence or talent rather than for the work they put in.

So, in conclusion, use rewards and sanctions wisely: they can be effective tools in your classroom management toolkit but they must be used correctly and cannot be the 'be all and end all' of behaviour management.

Part Five

Pedagogy and practice

Chapter Thirteen

Planning lessons

Curriculum instruction is most effective when it enables pupils to see various examples of how experts organise and solve problems, whereas curricula that focus on breadth of knowledge can prevent the effective organisation of knowledge because there is not enough time to learn in depth.

To kick-start our journey into pedagogy and practice, here are a few principles of effective curriculum design we should be mindful of…

1. The zone of proximal development

If the work is too easy, pupils will switch off; if the work is too hard, pupils will switch off. Therefore, work must be pitched in the 'struggle zone' – hard but achievable with support.

If something's too easy, we act habitually instead of thinking (e.g. 1 + 1 =); if it's too hard, we run out of processing power (e.g. 56 x 49237 =) and stop thinking. When we stop thinking, not only do we cease learning but we also become demotivated and reluctant to take on the next challenge. When we overcome a challenge and succeed, however, we are given the reward of dopamine, a pleasurable chemical which acts as a neurotransmitter and is a precursor of adrenaline and therefore a great motivator, encouraging us to take on the next challenge.

2. Desirable difficulties

Desirable difficulties make information harder to encode (learn initially) but easier to retrieve later. This leads to deeper learning. We achieve desirable difficulties by: spacing learning apart with increasingly long gaps; interleaving topics rather than finishing one topic then moving onto another; testing frequently – using low stakes quizzes at the start of topics/lessons to identify prior learning as well as knowledge gaps, and to interrupt forgetting; and making learning materials less clearly organised so that pupils have to think hard about the materials (e.g. using a difficult-to-read font).

3. Retrieval practice

At its simplest, learning is concerned with the interaction between our environment, our working memory and our long-term memory. Our working memory is about awareness and thinking; our long-term memory is about factual knowledge and procedural knowledge. We can improve the speed and ease with which we retrieve information from our long-term memory and transfer it into our working memory (where we can use it) by making connections between new and existing information – applying prior knowledge to new knowledge.

Prior knowledge helps us to 'chunk' information together, saving precious space in our limited working memory, allowing us to process more information. For example, the acronym 'BBC' takes one space in our working memory whereas, without the prior knowledge that the BBC is a TV company, the letters B, B and C would take three spaces. Prior knowledge is domain-specific. We know BBC whereas people in Japan would know WMBC. They'd take one space to remember WMBC whereas we would take four spaces to remember W, M, B and C. It is therefore important that we contextualise learning and link new learning to what pupils already know as well as to their life experiences.

4. Making learning 'stick'

Information 'sticks' when we use metaphor to relate new ideas to prior knowledge and to create images in pupils' minds. Information 'sticks' when we pique pupils' curiosity before we fill gaps in pupils' knowledge (thus convincing pupils they need the information). This can be done by asking pupils to make predictions or by setting a hypothesis to be proven or disproven. Information 'sticks' when we make abstract ideas concrete by grounding them in sensory reality (i.e. you make pupils feel something). The richer – sensorily and emotionally – new information is, the more strongly it is encoded in memory. And, finally, information 'sticks' when ideas are made credible by showing rather than telling pupils something (e.g. experiments, field studies, etc. beat textbooks for 'stickability').

Now let's bring all of these principles of curriculum design together and look at how we can build them into our lesson planning routines.

The five tenets of lesson planning

1. Well-planned lessons **connect the learning** in three ways: they articulate a clear learning goal that pupils understand, they articulate a clear purpose for the learning, and they ensure that pupils' starting points are identified through pre-tests.

2. Well-planned lessons **personalise the learning** by ensuring that the learning is tailored to meet individual needs and to match individual skills, interests, and styles; and by ensuring that this diagnostic data about pupils' starting points and misconceptions (both that gathered from pre-tests and that gleaned from on-going assessments) is used to inform the way the learning is planned.

3. Well-planned lessons **grab pupils' attentions** by ensuring that learning activities 'hook' pupils from the very beginning of the lesson by using sensory "hooks" and by ensuring that the learning is appropriately paced, and activities are appropriately varied and challenging.

4. Well-planned lessons **teach less so that pupils learn more** by covering a smaller amount of curriculum content but in far greater depth and detail – and from a range of different perspectives – than they would be able to achieve if they attempted to "get through" more content.

5. Well-planned lessons **make time for pupils to reflect** by providing pupils with regular opportunities to revisit their progress, to revise their thinking and to redraft their work, acting on the formative feedback they receive from teacher, peer and self-assessment.

With these tenets in mind, when planning lessons you should try to obey the following four rules…

The four rules of lesson planning

#1: Make it clear

Lesson plans should be focused on what pupils will think about rather than what they will do.

Although we are not naturally good thinkers, we do enjoy problem-solving – so we should frame our key messages (or lesson 'lead') around a problem to be solved or an enquiry to be investigated and answered.

First, we should decide what our vital 'take-away' messages are – rather than what will merely add hue and texture – then we should concentrate on writing questions rather than on creating fun activities.

Next, we should try to write a 'big question' which forms the basis for our lesson. Alternatively, we could pose a hypothesis to be proven or disproven.

#2: Make it satisfying

Piquing curiosity is key to effective teaching. Teachers tend to focus on imparting facts, but unless pupils know why those facts are important they are unlikely to retain them. Therefore, when planning lessons, we should make sure that before teaching our pupils the facts, we take time to pique their curiosity and make them realise why they need those facts.

The secret to convincing pupils that they need the information we intend to teach them is to start by highlighting the knowledge they are missing. Another technique is to start a lesson by asking pupils to make a prediction.

#3: Make it concrete

Another tip for planning learning is to ensure ideas 'stick' by making them tangible. Pupils find it hard to care about or understand abstract concepts. The more sensory 'hooks' we use, the better the ideas will stick.

Take, for example, Jane Elliott's famous 'blue-eyed/brown-eyed' experiment with third grade pupils the day after Martin Luther King had been assassinated in 1968. The purpose of the exercise was to teach her pupils the effects of belonging to a minority.

If pupils are made to care about something, they are made to feel something and this is an important part of the learning process because when we are exposed to new information we process it then attempt to connect it to existing information (in other words, we try to assimilate new knowledge with prior knowledge). The richer – sensorily and emotionally – the new information is, and the deeper the existing information is engrained, the more strongly new information will be encoded into memory.

When planning learning, therefore, we should try to obey the maxim "show don't tell" wherever possible. Telling our pupils something means we do all the work for them; showing them means they have to work for themselves.

#4: Make it real

Another useful strategy we could build into our lesson planning routine in order to make our big ideas "stick" is metaphor.

Metaphor is often considered the domain of English teachers, but the language of every school subject is rich with metaphor. Metaphor is good at making ideas stick because it brings ideas to life, it draws connections between new knowledge and existing knowledge.

For example, if you are trying to describe how electricity flows through a material, you'll need to explain the structure of atoms. You might first use a metaphor which describes atoms as "nature's building blocks" to help your pupils understand an atom's function. You will then need to explain how each atom is comprised of protons, which are positively charged, neutrons, which have no charge, and electrons, which are negatively charged. Then you would need to explain that, together, the protons and neutrons form the "nucleus" of the atom, and that the electrons travel around this nucleus. You might then use a metaphor which compares this "orbit" to the way the earth travels around the sun.

In each case, you are relating new information which pupils are unlikely to be able to process and therefore retain, with existing information (or prior knowledge) in order to help them imagine it, process it and retain it.

*

To conclude this chapter, let me issue a word of caution: Lessons should not take longer to plan than they do to teach and lesson plans should not be too bureaucratic because this only leads to prescription.

In short, if you've invested an hour or so producing a detailed lesson plan then you're much less likely to deviate from it when you need to and much more likely to stick slavishly to it in spite of the 'here and now' circumstances of your classroom.

So how can you ensure that your lesson planning routine remains manageable? One solution is to plan lessons backwards...

Plan lessons backwards

Planning lessons is the bane of many teachers' lives and a part of the job that's most likely to keep them up at night. Why is this? Well, one reason is that many teachers make the mistake of focusing their energies on designing amazing activities – things for pupils to do in the lesson which are engaging and fun. But, rather than looking at a blank sheet of paper and thinking up fun activities to fill it, you should start your lesson planning at the end – with the objective. By formulating your objective first, you are forced to ask yourself "What will pupils understand today?" (which is measurable) rather than "What will pupils do today?" (which is not).

A lesson activity can only be successful if it enables pupils to achieve the lesson's objective in a way that can be assessed – whether or not an activity is fun is of secondary importance if indeed not entirely irrelevant.

So here's a useful routine to establish when planning lessons…

When you plan a lesson, start by asking yourself: "Why am I teaching this?" and "What outcome do I desire?"

Then ask yourself: "How does this outcome relate to what I intend to teach tomorrow and the next day?"

And finally: "How does this outcome relate to what pupils need to learn by the end of this term/year/course?"

By building these questions into your lesson planning routine – repeated and reinforced every time you sit down to plan until it becomes a habit – you will stop planning each lesson in isolation, based on "fun" activities. Instead, you will start thinking about lessons as the small pieces of a large jigsaw – and each piece will develop ideas intentionally and incrementally while leading to the mastery of larger concepts.

Planning for the whole – for the medium-term rather than one lesson at a time – means methodically asking how each lesson will build on the previous lesson and prepare for the next.

It also means asking how this short sequence of lessons fits into a wider sequence which leads to mastery. This way, if you fail to achieve the previous day's objective, upon which tomorrow's objective depends, you simply go back and re-teach the content until pupils achieve mastery.

One final point: lesson plans shouldn't just focus on what the teacher will be doing but also on what pupils will be doing. This is not a contradiction: the objective must precede the activity and activities should not be deployed simply because they're fun.

You need to make sure your activities are meaningful and enable pupils to achieve your objective. Planning what your pupils will be doing is critical because it helps you to see the lesson through their eyes and this encourages you to find ways of keeping them productively engaged, thereby limiting instances of low-level disruption.

What pupils do in the classroom day after day is what they learn and become expert in. In other words, when making notes they're likely to forget the contents of their notes but remember the act of note-taking.

Therefore, we need to make sure that when we plan we remember that the activities pupils engage in will become inextricably bound up in their minds with the content of the lesson.

Chapter Fourteen

The importance of high expectations

Once you've planned a lesson, you need to teach it in such a way as to ensure that every pupil, no matter their starting point and prior attainment, is afforded the opportunity to produce their very best work. You need to ensure that your teaching is infused with high expectations of - and a bold ambition for - all your pupils, rather than placing an artificial ceiling in the way of their progress.

In short, *excellence* should be your by-word; *excellence* should come to define your classroom.

So what are high expectations and why are they important..?

The Pygmalion Effect

Robert Rosenthal and Lenore Jacobson conducted research in the 1960s which showed that when teachers expected an enhanced performance from their pupils, their pupils' performance was indeed enhanced. Their study supported the hypothesis – known as the Pygmalion Effect and named after a sculptor from Greek mythology who fell in love with one of his statues (Galatea) – that reality can be positively or negatively influenced by other people's expectations. In other words, the higher the expectations you have of somebody, the better they perform.

Rosenthal and Jacobson's research involved pupils in a Californian elementary school. They started by giving every pupil a covert IQ test. Without disclosing the scores, they gave the teachers the names of about 20 per cent of pupils chosen at random and told them that these chosen few were expected to do better than their classmates.

At the end of the study all the pupils were tested again using the same IQ test. Every pupil had increased their IQ scores. However, the chosen 20 per cent (chosen at random, remember) showed statistically significant gains. This led Rosenthal and Jacobson to conclude that teachers' expectations actually influenced pupil achievement. Or, to put it another way, teachers' biased expectancies affected reality and created self-fulfilling prophecies.

But why should this be? Well, Rosenthal believed that a teacher's attitude or mood positively affected his or her pupils because a teacher paid closer attention to so-called "gifted" pupils and treated them differently when they got stuck. For example, they were more willing to be patient and offer help when "gifted" pupils struggled because they believed that these pupils had the capacity to improve.

This led Rosenthal to predict that teachers subconsciously behave in ways that facilitate and encourage their pupils' success. In other words, teachers perpetrate the Pygmalion Effect: when they have high expectations of their pupils, their pupils perform well.

It follows, therefore, that having high expectations of pupils is not only a nice thing to do, it actually leads to improved performance. But saying and doing are two very different things. After all, what do high expectations actually look like in practice?

Well, as with most teaching strategies, having high expectations is simply about establishing a set of clear rules and routines. Doug Lemov shares a few such routines in his book, Teach Like a Champion.

For example, Lemov says that teachers who have high expectations operate a "No opt out" policy. In other words, a teaching sequence that begins with a pupil unable to answer a question should end with the same pupil answering that question as often as possible.

Lemov also says that teachers who have high expectations always insist that "Right is right". In other words, they set and defend a high standard of correctness in their classroom. For example...

They use simple positive language to express their appreciation of what a pupil has done and to express their expectation that he or she will now complete the task. For example: "You're almost there. Can you find the last piece?"

They insist that pupils answer the question they have asked not a different question entirely. These teachers are clear that the right answer to any question other than the one they have asked is, by definition, wrong.

As well as insisting on the right answer, teachers with high expectations insist that pupils answer the right question at the right time. They protect the integrity of their lesson by not jumping ahead to engage an exciting right answer at the wrong time.

These teachers insist their pupils use precise, technical vocabulary.

Lemov says that teachers who have high expectations "Stretch it". In other words, a sequence of learning does not end with a right answer; these teachers reward right answers with follow-up questions that extend knowledge and test for reliability.

For example, they ask how or why, ask for another way to answer, ask for a better word, ask for evidence, ask pupils to integrate a related skill, and/or ask pupils to apply the same skill in a new setting.

Lemov says that, for the teachers who have high expectations of their pupils, "format matters". In other words, it is not just what their pupils say that matters but how they say it. To succeed, pupils must take their knowledge and express it in the language of opportunity.

Pupils' attitudes

As well as having high expectations of our pupils, we should insist that our pupils have high expectations of themselves, because only by believing in yourself and in your own ability to get better will you actually do so. So what does this look like in practice?

First, pupils should have a growth mindset and believe that they can get better at anything if they work hard. This means having a thirst for knowledge, this means accepting that work needs to be drafted and redrafted, and this means following the maxim that if it isn't excellent, it isn't finished (never settling for work that is less than their best). This also means setting aspirational goals for themselves and expecting to achieve them.

Second, pupils should embrace challenge and enjoy hard work because they know it will help them to learn. This means actively engaging in lessons and readily accepting any new challenges that are presented. It also means exerting a lot of effort and engaging in deliberate practice. It means pushing themselves in lessons, practising something over and over again, and regarding additional study opportunities such as homework as an important way of consolidating and deepening their learning rather than as an onerous chore.

Third, pupils should seek out and welcome feedback. They should value other people's opinions and advice and use it to help them improve their work. Feedback should be given and received with kindness in a manner that is helpful and not unduly critical, and yet it should be constructive and specific about what needs to be improved.

Fourth, pupils should be resilient. By being resilient – not giving up easily when things get hard – they will overcome obstacles. Moreover, they will be happy to make mistakes because they know they will learn from them. In practice, this means that pupils ask good questions in order to further their learning, this means pupils always try and solve problems for themselves before asking others for help.

Finally, pupils should be inspired by other people's success. They should seek out examples of great work, discovering what makes it great then using this knowledge to inform their own work. They should take collective responsibility for the work of the class and have a vested interest in everyone's success.

This means that pupils support each other and encourage each other to succeed. This means that pupils work well in groups and are confident expressing their views and sharing their ideas. This means that pupils are good at giving each other feedback that is kind, specific and helpful.

The Golem Effect

To summarise, the Pygmalion Effect is important because it gives teachers a reason to believe that having high expectations of their pupils actually helps them to perform better. But here's a word of warning…

The opposite of the Pygmalion Effect is the Golem Effect – if we expect our pupils to perform badly, chances are they will. Both the Pygmalion Effect and the Golem Effect have their downsides: they are self-fulfilling prophecies in part because they encourage us to find evidence that supports our expectations regardless of whether or not such evidence exists.

In other words, we are in danger of interpreting pupils' performances in line with what we think they will achieve rather than accurately and based on evidence. If we have high expectations of a pupil then we are more inclined to think they are performing well, irrespective of whether or not they actually are. Equally, if we have low expectations of a pupil we are eager to find evidence that they are performing badly and seize on the slightest sign of it.

This is sometimes called the observer-expectancy effect and is the situation by which a researcher's cognitive bias causes them to unconsciously influence the participants of an experiment.

Confirmation biases such as this can lead to the experimenter interpreting results incorrectly because of their tendency to look for information that conforms to their hypothesis, while overlooking information that argues against it.

So as a new teacher you should have high expectations of all your pupils because this will encourage them to perform better. Moreover, it will help them to develop high expectations of themselves, and if they believe in themselves they are more likely to succeed.

But beware of false prophets: use empirical evidence to help you determine a pupil's actual performance; be attuned to your natural tendency to find evidence that supports your beliefs, regardless of whether such evidence is accurate or fair.

Chapter Fifteen

Establishing high expectations

In the previous chapter we established why high expectations were important and began to explore what this might actually look and sound like in practice.

In this chapter we'll examine four rules and routines for establishing and embedding the right attitudes to learning in your classroom…

*

Aristotle once said that "excellence is not an act but a habit", and so it is with teaching: the foundations of a successful classroom are built of rules and routines, regularly repeated and reinforced. Rules may not be as sexy as, say, neuroscience, but without these essential groundworks the edifice of learning would simply crumble.

With this in mind, it is important that you firmly and frankly set out your rules on day one, immediately establishing who's boss – because if you don't articulate clear dos and don'ts before you start teaching then you will find it difficult to break the bad habits that inevitably fill the void.

Let's start by exploring four 'entry-level' rules and routines…

1. Always have a seating plan

You should always have a seating plan for every class you teach, adapted for every classroom you teach in. A seating plan serves two purposes: first, it helps you to learn the names of your pupils because seating them where you want gives you a useful reference point; second, it helps establish your authority in the room by dictating who sits with whom, forbidding the formation of friendship groups – and in so doing, it makes clear that your lesson is a place for learning not for socialising.

If you do not have a seating plan, pupils will naturally sit next to their friends and, no matter how honourable their intentions, will find it hard to resist the urge to talk. When groups of friends congregate, there's a danger that the social divisions that exist outside your classroom will be perpetuated. Your classroom should be a safe haven, a warm and welcoming environment in which every pupil feels valued, respected and encouraged to participate in learning.

When given the freedom of choice, the less attentive pupils in a class tend to gravitate towards the back where they can avoid detection. Therefore, without a seating plan, more eager pupils are likely to surge ahead while less eager pupils fall further and further behind.

So how should you design your seating plan? The answer is: it depends on what you want to achieve and what you are planning to do in your lesson.

A safe starting point is to seat pupils in alphabetical order, perhaps alternating boy-girl-boy-girl. This will help you to learn pupils' names and there is a good chance it will split most friendships up too. If you have free reign over the layout of your room, go with the default position: rows of desks – split into pairs – all facing the front of the room. This makes it easier for you to ensure that everyone is on task and makes it easier for your pupils to see you and the board.

Later, you may want to use your knowledge of pupils' progress to guide you, perhaps seating pupils of similar abilities together so that you can target your interventions, supporting those pupils who need it the most while also differentiating the work you set.

Or you might seat higher ability pupils next to their lower ability peers in order to encourage the practice of peer-teaching. One further consideration is behaviour: as you get to know how your pupils behave, you might decide to place the naughtiest pupils nearest to you.

Whatever your rationale, insist on 100 per cent compliance at all times. Do not allow any pupil – no matter the circumstances – to negotiate a move. That way madness lies!

2. Learn their names and make a connection

My second piece of advice is to learn your pupils' names as quickly as you can and use their names as often as you can. Ask pupils if they have a preferred name or (clean, sensible) nickname. You will be surprised how powerful this can be in making them feel valued.

As well as using your seating plan to help you, you could also ask pupils to wear a name tag or display one on their desks. Alternatively, you could ask pupils to say their names each time they contribute to class discussion. You will only need to do this for a week or so.

In addition to using pupils' names, make a connection by showing an interest in their hobbies and interests, enquiring about their weekends and evening activities.

If they play for a school team, find out how they fared last week and offer your congratulations or commiserations.

Make a connection with their parents, too, by phoning home as often as possible – try to make it a habit to instigate a handful of phone calls each week. Use the calls to give an update on progress, to praise hard work, or to raise parents' awareness of any behavioural or academic issues.

Making this effort really pays off over time, particularly when you encounter behaviour or attainment problems later.

3. Set clear expectations

While we are talking about praising or rebuking pupils, try to strike a positive balance whereby you reward good behaviour or effort three times more often than you sanction unacceptable performance.

Where possible, signpost the right actions as a means of highlighting and correcting the wrong ones. For example, instead of saying "take your coat off" or "stop talking and look at me", say

"I can see that John has taken his coat off and that Jenny is facing this way waiting for me to start".

And there's never any harm in engaging in a bit of shameless sycophancy: tell every class that they're your favourites and that you really love teaching them! Share a little about yourself, too; if they see you as a human being, they are less likely to enjoy angering or upsetting you. Bear-baiting is less fun if the bear's a really nice guy who regularly shows you photographs of his wife and kids!

When you need to sanction a pupil, make sure you hold firm. Always follow the school's behaviour policy and do not allow pupils to negotiate with you or argue about the unfairness of life. Be strong and resolute. Pupils will sense a weakness if you waver and they will not respect your authority if you back down or don't see your threats through to the bitter end.

Always be prepared to do whatever you say you are going to do. As such, avoid unrealistic or unfair sanctions that punish you as much as they punish the pupil. Pupils will feel just as aggrieved by a 10-minute detention as they will by a half-hour detention.

Always try to sanction the pupil who misbehaved rather than the whole class. Avoid at all costs any form of collective punishment because pupils always, and rightly, consider these to be grossly unfair.

You should also strive to be consistent and fair in what misdemeanours you sanction pupils for. Set out a list of class rules (or collaboratively agree these with pupils – they nearly always propose the same rules you would wish to establish, particularly if you steer them in the right direction).

Here are some suggested class rules that you might adopt and/or adapt:
- You must enter the classroom quickly and quietly and take the seat you have been assigned.
- You must arrive to lessons with the right equipment.
- You must follow your teacher's instructions – they not you are in charge of the room.
- You must listen when other people are speaking.

- You must not call out. Put your hand up if you want to speak.
- You must not get up from your seat or leave the room without permission.
- You must complete all work to the best of your ability and hand it in on time.
- You must extend good manners to everyone at all times.

4. Establish clear routines for the beginnings and ends of lessons

You can make or break a lesson in the first few minutes. You need to establish your authority and show them that your classroom is your domain. Make pupils line-up outside – at least for the first lesson – and only enter once they are silent, attentive, and have removed their coats.

Once pupils have embedded the behaviours you expect for entering your classroom and sitting down, you might want to have tasks readily displayed on the board or on desks so that pupils can get started as soon as they enter. You should always greet pupils at the door where possible, and do so with a smile and quick greeting.

The best starter work is that which reviews, consolidates or builds on the work completed in the previous lesson or lessons, and that which is differentiated and requires pupils to revisit or revise work they had previously found difficult.

Whatever approach you decide upon for the start of your lessons, always try to be in your classroom before your pupils and have your resources ready to go. Have a lesson planned in advance and make sure you know what you are talking about. If pupils think you are more disorganised than they are, they won't respect you or trust you to help them make progress.

Set out clear expectations for the end of lessons, too, and manage them just as keenly as you do the beginning: you are in charge and only you can say when the lesson has finished and pupils can pack away.

Rehearse how to do this calmly and quietly until this becomes automatic. Establish routines for who leaves first in order to avoid having a mad rush out of the door. If you need to speak to pupils at the end, do so quickly so as not to impair the start of the lesson for their next teacher.

*

The habit of cooperation

The essential groundworks of effective teaching are built of rules and routines, regularly repeated and reinforced.

Teaching is an art and, as with all art forms, it relies on the mastery and application of a set of fundamental skills.

So let's now take a look at how to establish good habits and routines for undertaking everyday tasks – such as handing out work – in order to reduce low-level disruption…

When setting and enforcing rules and routines, it is often tempting to focus on the big things. After all, it is hard to ignore a flagrant flouting of the rules without losing face.

But the silent killer in the classroom is low-level disruption – those seemingly minor distractions like tapping a pen, swinging on a chair, chewing gum, drawing graffiti in an exercise book, and so on.

Low-level disruption is what really stymies learning because it wages a war of attrition; it corrodes the edifice of good practice you have worked so hard to construct. The best way to deal with low-level disruption is to remember that it is not (usually) intended to undermine you, it is just a cheap form of entertainment. So keep your cool.

Quickly take the names of the perpetrators without making a scene or stemming the flow of learning, then sanction them after the lesson – but do not ignore it or it will spread like a virulent weed.

Most low-level disruption arises during transitions, during those moments in which mundane everyday tasks are performed and there is a lull in the pace of learning.

It would follow, therefore, that to embed good routines for managing those transitions is – at least in part – to obviate low-level disruption. So let's take a look at a few such routines…

Handing out books

Take the distribution and collection of classroom materials. If you explicitly teach your pupils how to pass out papers on the first day of school – taking a minute or so to explain the right way to do it (e.g. pass across rows, start on the teacher's command, only the person passing papers can get out of his or her seat, do it in silence, etc.), then allowing pupils 10 to 15 minutes to practise it, although it may distract you from the curriculum for half an hour at the start of the year, it will pay dividends over time, saving you time and energy every lesson for the rest of the year and limiting the opportunity for pupils to engage in low-level disruption.

If an average class passes papers back and forth 20 times a day and it typically takes 90 seconds to do so, imagine how much time you will save if a class got so much better at doing it through practice that it only took them

30 seconds. That's 20 minutes a day! Just think how much time you will save each term and each year, and how productively you could use that time. And just think how little time your pupils will now have to engage in low-level disruption.

So establish early on how you want books to be handed out and get your pupils to practise this everyday exercise over and over until they get it right. Make this rehearsal a competition to see how quickly they can do it, setting a target time and praising them when they achieve it.

*

As well as practising handing out work, it is worth rehearsing some of the other seemingly inconsequential activities that take place every lesson, such as transitioning from one task to another, engaging in paired talk and group work, taking part in questions-and-answers, and so on.

These activities are the glue that binds your classroom together and the oil that greases its wheels. As such, it is crucial you get them right, so you'd be advised not to leave them to chance.

Turn-taking

Establish rules and routines for paired talk such as how to take turns, make notes, give feedback to the class, comment on other pairs' answers, and so on.

Team work

Likewise, practise how to work as part of a group, reinforcing what's expected of pupils – for example, any member of the group could be asked to give feedback so every pupil must be prepared.

Question and answer

Perhaps the most important routine to practise, however, is how to engage in whole-class question-and-answer sessions: make clear your rules around no-hands-up (questions will be targeted at named individuals and no-one must call out) and no-excuses (everyone must give an answer, "I don't know" is not acceptable), and practise routines such as commenting on and adding to someone else's answer in a polite and constructive manner.

Study skills

As well as rehearsing classroom drills and habits, practise frequently used study skills such as skimming and scanning texts, taking notes, mind-mapping, etc. Again, dedicating time at the start of the year to developing these skills will pay off over time.

Marking and feedback

Another routine to get right from the very beginning is marking. You will need to condition pupils in the art of self, peer and teacher assessment.

Make clear that pupils have to mark their own work for spelling and punctuation before they submit it for peer or teacher assessment, and make clear what you will and will not mark, what you do and do not find acceptable in terms of presentation and accuracy.

Set out clear ground rules such as: work that is not handed in on time will not be marked and the pupil will be given a detention, work that is illegible or does not have a name on it will not be marked, work that contains basic errors will not be marked and will have to be rewritten, etc.

As with all the rules and routines in this book, it is absolutely vital that you expect 100 per cent compliance and do not give in to the temptation to "let that one go". It is a war of attrition, but you will win it one battle at a time.

And finally...

Remember you are not alone. Your classroom may well be your kingdom and it may well be built on your rules and routines, but nevertheless your kingdom is just one in a league of nations and you are just citizen of the wider world of the school.

For your part, make sure you follow the school rules and obey their policies, you owe it to your colleagues to hold the party line. For their part, your colleagues should support you and advise you. Don't be afraid to ask for help and advice

Part Six

Assessment and feedback

Chapter Sixteen

Marking

One common misconception about teaching is that teachers must mark every word written by their pupils. This isn't true and even Ofsted - who were often blamed for perpetuating this mentality - now make it clear that teachers, departments and schools should work SMART when it comes to strategically marking and assessing pupil work.

Getting pupils more involved in marking their learning (self- and peer- assessment) and utilising creative and visually-stimulating marking strategies is embraced in many schools.

So if marking is not about poring over and judging every word written by pupils, what is it? What does effective marking look like in practice?

I find it useful to refer to a mnemonic which summarises seven features of effective marking...

A mnemonic for MARKING

Think of effective assessment in terms of the mnemonic MARKING where the letters stand for...

M = Mark constructively, regularly and fairly
A = Assess formatively and summatively
R = Record progress
K = Keep pupils and parents informed
I = Individualise comments and targets
N = Note the gaps in learning
G = Guide planning

Mark constructively, regularly and fairly

You should **mark constructively**. This means marking for improvement not marking for failure. In other words, you shouldn't simply cross out mistakes or circle errors; they should highlight – explicitly - those areas that the pupil could improve upon, expand or develop.

Work should be marked against clearly explained success criteria and the purpose of the marking should be focused. In other words, if the purpose of a piece of writing is to help pupils improve their use of, say, rhetorical devices, and the teacher has not also made clear that the work is being marked for spelling, then spelling mistakes should be overlooked (or at least marked with a light touch – perhaps the odd basic mistake could be identified or corrected but most other mistakes tactically ignored) and the teacher's comments should focus on how well the pupil has used rhetorical devices and how the pupil could improve their use of rhetorical devices (with examples) not on other matters such as presentation or grammar.

Each area for improvement you identify should be accompanied by some suggestions of how to improve, perhaps with examples the pupil could use as a starting point. The pupil should certainly have a clear idea about how they can improve their work once they've read your comments. And, moreover, the pupil should feel positive about the progress they've made and about the further progress that lies ahead, not downhearted or demoralised by your pedantic criticisms!

You should **mark regularly**. Marking regularly not only helps teachers to manage their workload, it helps pupils to see the progress they're making, encourages them to make further progress, and helps them to see the value of their work – and to see that it is valued by the teacher.

Regular marking also reinforces the importance of completing work on time and presenting it neatly - it gives pupils' work a real audience. If pupils know that their work is rarely marked, they are less inclined to complete it or to meet the deadlines the teacher sets. Equally, pupils will spend less time on their work if they feel it will most likely be ignored.

You should **mark fairly**. Marking fairly means marking work consistently, marking work against the success criteria that you shared with the class beforehand and marking work according to the level each pupil is working at and aiming for.

To mark fairly, therefore, is not the same as marking every pupil according to the same standards. Your marking should be differentiated according to the individual pupils' needs and abilities. Your marks should be consistent with the expectations placed upon each pupil – not consistent across an entire class or year group.

If a pupil is currently at a grade 4, say, and is targeted a grade 5 by the end of the Year 11 – whereas most of the class are expected to achieve a grade 6 – then he or she should be marked according to the progress he or she has made towards achieving a grade 5, not against the progress they have made towards achieving the class average grade 6 (or indeed any other targets such as the national average).

Equally, just because one pupil has exceeded his or her target of, say, a grade 7, does not mean you should encourage them to rest on their laurels; you should now comment on what they need to do to achieve a grade 8 and 9.

Assess formatively and summatively

Formative assessment is about helping pupils to make progress by identifying which aspects of their work they could improve upon, whereas summative assessment is a straightforward summary of what a pupil has already achieved.

That's not to say that summative assessment isn't also important. For example, summative tests can be used formatively.

Firstly, you can use formative strategies to help pupils prepare for summative tests.

Secondly, you can use summative tests as a means of identifying learning targets from the detailed evidence that summative test questions can produce.

Pupils should certainly be encouraged to reflect on the work they have done to enable them to revise effectively. Pupils could traffic-light test questions to identify where their understanding is secure and where they need to concentrate their efforts. The traffic lights can form a revision plan with pupils being asked to identify questions on past examination papers which test their 'amber' or 'red' areas. This provides pupils with focus so that they concentrate on their areas of weakness rather than simply reviewing everything they already know.

Pupils could also prepare their own examination questions and mark each other's answers, a process which helps pupils to understand the examination process and focus on improvement. Classes could also engage in peer-marking of test papers. Teachers can set and mark summative tests to provide pupils with experience of examinations and to practice their learning.

In short, summative assessment is still useful to teachers and pupils but only when it is used formatively. Therefore, summative tests should be seen as a positive part of the learning process, used to help chart pupils' learning rather than to dominate their learning. Allowing pupils to be actively involved in the testing process can help them to see that they are the beneficiaries rather than the victims of testing!

Record progress

When you mark pupils' work, it is important that you identify and record the progress the pupils have made. In other words, you should join the dots between the pupils' past achievements and their current achievements in order to show that they are making progress – however slowly – and that they are improving on their past performance. This helps motivate pupils because they can see that they are getting better, they are learning and performing better than they did before.

Often, pupils can be downhearted by graded work because grades show that they still haven't met their target or that they are performing poorly in comparison with their peers. In a mixed ability class where some pupils always achieve grade 5s and above, the pupil who never gets above a grade 4 is bound to feel demoralised and wonder what the point of working hard really is. But a grade 4 may represent a real success for that pupil. A grade 4 may mark real progress.

Only by joining the dots and recording that progress – and then celebrating it – can EVERY pupil see that they have achieved something.

If work is marked regularly and fairly then it should show progress. Marking records should show the journey a pupil is making from their starting position (the scaled score or grade they achieved at the end of the last year or key stage) to their final destination (their target mark or grade). Although a pupil may not have achieved their target grade or a grade they are happy with, they may have improved on their previous mark/grade and this should be recorded and then rewarded.

You should also take notice of the overall picture which shows to what extent and how quickly the whole class is making progress. If the level and speed of progress demonstrated by the class is not what you expect it to be, then perhaps it's time to reconsider your approach.

Keep pupils and parents informed

As above, pupils should be kept informed of the progress they are making and be made to feel good about the effort they are exerting (and be encouraged to exert more effort). Equally, pupils need to know when they are falling short of what is expected of them. Feedback should be specific - pointing out in clear, concise terms what the pupil needs to do in order to improve; and feedback should be focused - sticking to the most important aspects of a pupil's work and not overloading a pupil with too much information so that the key messages are lost.

Parents need to be kept informed, too, if they are to support the pupil and the school. They need to know why their child isn't performing as well as they should/could and what they can do to help. The school should involve parents as soon as possible and as often as possible, allowing them time and opportunity to do something about it, not when it is too late to act.

Nothing you say at a parents' evening should come as a huge shock to a pupil's parents: they should have a general picture of how well their son or daughter is doing. Regular contact with parents, though time-consuming, will pay dividends in the long-term.

Individualise comments and targets

It is important that your comments are personal; that your comments refer specifically to an individual pupil's work and are not generalised comments about the nature of the task they have completed. Often, comments simply repeat what pupils already know: the learning objectives or the success criteria. Pupils learn nothing from this. Comments should refer to the pupil's work and should provide the pupil with specific, detailed advice about what they can do to improve. Suggestions for improvement need to be helpful – teachers need to provide examples of what the pupil can do, not simply state that they need to do better.

Targets should be bespoke, too. Targets should be based on a pupil's past performance, on what they do well and what they need to improve in order to fulfil their potential. Targets should be negotiated with pupils so that pupils understand what is expected of them and take personal ownership. Pupils need to know how they can close the gap between their current performance and their desired performance.

Note the gaps in learning

Assessment is not solely for the pupil's benefit. You should use your assessments to help them identify what pupils do and do not know, what they have and have not learnt. Assessments may point to gaps in pupils' learning. This may help you to decide what you need to teach next, or may indicate that something you've already taught has not been learnt and therefore needs to be revisited. Once the gaps in pupils' learning have been identified, they should help to guide your future planning...talking of which...

Guide planning

You need to view your lesson plans and schemes of work as flexible, fluid constructions not as being set in stone. All teaching plans should act as rough guides to what needs to be taught; you should never stick to your plans rigidly because to do so is to belie the fact that pupils are human, that pupils are individuals!

Deviations and tangents are not always a bad thing…they can take you and your pupils in interesting and illuminating directions which you had not anticipated before the lesson began but which support or extend the learning. Some aspects of your lesson plan may not take as long as you had predicted because pupils simply 'get it' (either because they have learnt it before, your teaching is clearer than you think, or because of some innate ability your class possess which allows them to process the information easily). Equally, some aspects of your lesson plan may take much longer than you'd predicted.

And so, just as you might veer off plan when it becomes clear that pupils are finding the work too easy and are growing bored, or when it becomes clear that pupils are struggling with the work and are growing demoralised; you must also veer off plan – or alter and adapt the plan – when the results of your assessments tell you to do so.

When your assessments suggest that pupils haven't understood the work, it is important to take note of this finding, not just put it down to experience and promise to do better next year. Equally, when your assessments suggest that pupils have excelled at an aspect of their work, you should reflect on your teaching plans in order to identify what went well (and can be repeated) and how the success can be harnessed in the future.

Chapter Seventeen

Giving feedback

Once you or your pupils have marked their work (obeying the principles contained in the mnemonic MARKING), the process should naturally lead to the giving of formative feedback so that the pupil knows what they have mastered and what they still need to practice and perfect…

Feedback works best when it is explicit about the marking criteria, offers suggestions for improvement, and is focused on how pupils can close the gap between their current and their desired performance; it does not focus on presentation or quantity of work. Be warned: feedback can backfire – it needs to cause a cognitive rather than emotional reaction – i.e. it should cause thinking. It should, therefore, avoid personal criticisms or listing too many areas for improvement, and instead focus on the work (not the pupil) and on a small number of key improvements (marginal gains, if you will).

Ultimately, though, the only useful feedback is that which is acted upon – it is crucial that the teacher knows the pupil and knows when and what kind of feedback to give, then plans time for pupils to act on feedback (e.g. DIRT - directed improvement and reflection time).

Giving effective formative feedback

Research has shown that the most influential form of feedback is verbal. However, with the possible exception of practical subjects, teachers rarely get the opportunity to have quality one-to-one dialogue with pupils during lessons.

Pupil-to-pupil verbal feedback, therefore, is a vital element of classroom feedback. Self-, paired- and group-assessment of work against set criteria - and against grade exemplars of pupils' work - enables pupils to analyse work objectively and motivates them to take control of their own progress. To be able to self- pair- or group-assess work, though, pupils need to know what the difference between grades is. Without explicit knowledge of what makes, say, a grade 5 and grade 6 piece of work, pupils are simply guessing at how to make progress. So some preparation work needs to be done before you can harness the power of pupil-to-pupil feedback. But time spent training pupils to give feedback will pay off over the long-term.

In addition to planning for peer-feedback, it is worth teachers planning opportunities for ongoing individual dialogue between teachers and pupils – this is likely to take place at the end of a unit or module. Try to build in some time for one-to-one feedback to pupils, perhaps whilst the rest of the class are redrafting work.

Let's take a deeper look at how to make self- and peer-assessment work in your classroom…

Self- and peer- assessment

First some definitions…

Peer-assessment is when pupils engage in a constructively critical way with others about the quality of work and how to improve it. Peer-assessment provides pupils with valuable feedback, enabling them to learn from and support each other. It also adds a valuable dimension to learning: the opportunity to talk, discuss, explain and challenge each other enables pupils to achieve more than they could unaided.

Self-assessment is when one pupil pin-points their own current level of performance and determines what needs to be done to improve. Self-assessment promotes independent learning, helping pupils to take increasing responsibility for their own progress.

Self- and peer-assessment are important teaching tools because:
- They give pupils a greater responsibility for their learning
- They allow pupils to help and be helped by their friends
- Using these strategies encourages pupils to work collaboratively with others and to reflect upon their own performance – two valuable life-skills
- Using them means everyone benefits from each other's comments and suggestions

- They help pupils to realise their true potential
- They enable pupils to see the progress they are making
- Pupils can begin to work out for themselves how to improve their work
- They enable teachers to teach more effectively

So how do they work in practice..?

Self-assessment

Teachers can introduce self-assessment in three steps:

1. Firstly, pupils should be encouraged to identify their successes. If the learning objective is clear (for example, it identifies a knowledge, skill or concept) then pupils can simply underline the evidence of their success. This kind of self-assessment leads to greater levels of self-esteem and motivation.

2. Next, pupils can identify an area of improvement. As well as underlining a success (measured against the learning objective), pupils can find one aspect of their work which could be improved, perhaps by drawing a dotted line underneath it. The teacher can then write a suggestion of how the work can be improved.

3. Finally, pupils are now in a position to identify their successes, highlight an area for improvement and make the improvement without help from the teacher. The work is then handed to the teacher with the success highlighted, an area for improvement highlighted and an improvement made.

Using clear success criteria in your lessons is also conducive to self-assessment. If the success criteria are closed (in other words, they have right or wrong answers) then the self-assessment can be a simple 'yes or no' exercise. When the success criteria are open (in other words, they are about making quality judgments), then the self-assessment is focused around those elements of the success criteria which need improving. This is also when exemplar modelling is useful.

Using traffic lights can be helpful in self-assessment tasks. Pupils can RAG their work: *green* means the success criteria have been met; *amber* means they have been partially met; and *red* means they have not been met and the pupil needs assistance. Traffic lights work best when pupils are learning facts rather than skills because making simple judgments about the extent to which a skill has been learnt can be problematic.

Peer-assessment

Peer-assessment can be anything from pupils helping each other to improve a piece of work to a longer process of analysing whole pieces of work and giving detailed feedback.

Peer-assessment is uniquely valuable for several reasons: firstly, peer-assessment improves motivation and encourages pupils to work more carefully; secondly, peer-assessment involves giving and receiving feedback in a language which pupils understand - they can convey meaning to those still struggling better than many teachers can, and pupils can accept criticisms from each other better than they can from the teacher; thirdly, feedback from a pair or group to the teacher can command more attention than feedback given by an individual pupil, and so strengthens pupil voice.

Peer-assessment can also help pupils to self-assess because reading each other's work provides pupils with a similar kind of opportunity to that which teachers are afforded at standardisation meetings. It helps them, through exemplification, to engage with what a particular grade looks like in practice and also enables them to see how a piece of work might be approached. Seeing how someone else has tackled the same task helps pupils to reflect on their own performance.

For peer-assessment to take place, teachers need to create a safe environment in which pupils feel comfortable having others read their work. Teachers can encourage collaboration and the sharing of work and ideas by allowing their own performance to be critiqued and by modelling good feedback, both in the way they talk to the class and through their written comments. Pupils need to see examples of good practice to be able to know what to do themselves.

It is useful to establish some rules for peer-assessment such as:

- Both pupils should be taught how to assess work
- Both pupils should have a similar level of ability
- Both pupils need sufficient time to reflect on each other's work before giving feedback
- Both pupils should begin with a positive comment when giving feedback
- Both pupils should agree on the areas for improvement before sharing or formalising them

Once work has been peer-assessed, it should be returned to the owner so that they can add their own comments and make any improvements that have been identified before the work is passed to the teacher. The teacher should then add to what has already been commented on, giving weight to the self- and peer-assessment rather than ignoring it and marking it as if for the first time.

Let's take a look in more detail at one popular method of peer-assessment and feedback…

Gallery critique

In gallery critique, which is a form of peer assessment, the work of every pupil is displayed on boards or photocopied for all to read. Pupils start by looking at the work silently before giving comments and the focus is predominantly positive. Pupils select examples from the gallery that impress them and then discuss why.

There are three rules for gallery critique. Feedback should be:

1. Kind,
2. Specific, and
3. Helpful.

Here are some useful guidelines:

- Begin with the author/designer of the work explaining his/her ideas and goals, and explaining what aspects of the work he/she is seeking help with.

- Critique the work not the person.
- Begin with something positive then move on to constructive criticism.
- Use "I" statements wherever possible (e.g. "I'm confused by this…" rather than "This makes no sense").
- Use questions wherever possible (e.g. "Have you considered…" rather than "You need to…").

The rules should always be obeyed; the guidelines should usually – but not always – apply.

It is important to differentiate between critiquing for specific content qualities and critiquing for conventions. It is also important to focus on vocabulary-building – avoiding general comments like "it's good" or "it's bad"; instead commenting forensically on the work.

The best feedback

The most effective form of feedback is 'comment only'. In other words, the best feedback is that which informs pupils what they need to do in order to improve, rather than that which simply awards them a mark or grade.

We'll look at comment-only feedback in the next chapter…

Chapter Eighteen

Using comment-only feedback

An essential part of formative assessment is giving feedback to pupils, both to assess their current achievement and to indicate what their next steps should be. However, traditional forms of feedback – grading every piece of work, rewarding good grades with merits, etc. - lead to regression rather than progression in pupils' achievements.

Why should this be?

Firstly, marking or grading every piece of pupils' work can cause pupils to become complacent or demoralised: pupils who continually receive grades of, say, an 8 or higher can become complacent whereas pupils who continually receive grades of, say, a 4 or lower can become demoralised.

Secondly, marks or grades can lead pupils to compare themselves with other pupils and to focus on their image and status rather than be encouraged to think about their work and how they can improve it. Grades also focus pupils' attentions on their ability rather than on the importance of effort, damaging their self-esteem.

By contrast, a number of studies have shown that, when feedback is given in the form of comments only (with marks or grades reserved for the end of a unit or module) pupils' levels of motivation and attainment go up. Comments which focus on how pupils can improve encourage pupils to believe that they can improve.

In 2000, The University of Bristol's 'LEARN' project carried out a series of interviews with over 200 pupils from Years 3 to 13. Pupils were asked about how they responded to various kinds of feedback. The project's key findings were as follows:

- Pupils were often confused by effort and attainment grades
- Pupils occasionally felt that their effort was not recognised by their teachers
- Pupils preferred regular, verbal feedback to written feedback at the end of a unit
- Pupils were often unable to act on their teachers' feedback effectively
- Pupils felt that constructive feedback – that which was critical - helped them to improve their performance

In 1998, Ruth Butler conducted a controlled study in which she gave feedback to pupils in three groups of a similar age and ability. She gave each group a different kind of feedback: she gave the first group feedback in the form of marks or grades; she gave the second group comment-only feedback; and she gave the third group marks or grades alongside comments.

Butler's study found that progress (measured in the form of improved exam results) was greater for pupils in the comment-only group, with the other two groups showing no real progress at all. Even when the comments that accompanied grades were positive, discussions with pupils showed they thought the teacher was just 'being kind' and that the grade was the real indicator of the quality of their work not the comment.

This is not to suggest that ALL comment-only marking is effective or preferable to awarding marks and grades. The content of the comments is also central to their success…

In Formative Assessment in the Secondary Classroom, Shirley Clarke suggested that teachers tend to give written feedback on four main elements of a pupil's work:

1. Presentation;
2. Quantity;
3. Accuracy of spelling, punctuation and grammar; and
4. Effort.

Although these aspects are important, teachers are guilty of over-emphasising them to the extent that the main focus of the lesson is side-lined.

Rather than focusing on these four elements, effective feedback involves being explicit about the marking criteria. Suggestions for improvement should be focused on how pupils can close the gap between their current performance and the performance they are targeted to achieve, and suggestions should also be relevant to the lesson or unit and refer to the learning objectives.

It is important that teachers give pupils examples of how they can close the gap. In other words, teachers cannot simply say "improve his sentence"; they must explain ways in which it can be improved.

Feedback which simply reiterates the learning objective (such as "Say more about…", "Give more detail on…", "Redo this…") are unhelpful because they only act as a reminder of what the pupil has already been told. Feedback which involves the teacher giving examples and ideas (such as "Say more about… such as 'How much..?', 'When did...?', "Give more detail…for instance 'What else..?', 'In what ways..?'" and "Redo this…you could use…") are more effective because they provide scaffolding. Teachers could even share some models of what the pupil might write. The pupil can then be invited to choose one of these models or write their own example.

Of course, what pupils do with our comments is also important. Providing pupils with comments about how to improve and then moving on to the next topic is clearly fruitless. Black and Wiliam found that "for assessment to be formative, the feedback information has to be used". In other words, pupils need to be afforded the time and opportunity required to act on the feedback. A valuable approach is to devote some lesson time to redrafting one or two pieces of work, so that emphasis can be placed on feedback for improvement within a supportive environment. This can change pupils' expectations about the purposes of class-work and home-work, not to mention the purposes of teachers' comments. All the research into what makes formative assessment effective also emphasises the importance of involving the pupil in the process. Therefore, teachers need to model effective marking and feedback strategies so that pupils can train to be effective self- and peer-assessors.

Of course, giving feedback in the form of comments rather than marks or grades takes more time so teachers need to find ways of managing the extra workload. For example, teachers might spend more time marking certain pieces of work to ensure that they can provide good feedback. In order to make time for this, teachers might not mark some other pieces, might mark only a third of pupils' books each week or might involve pupils in checking simpler tasks through self- and/or peer-assessment. And perhaps, to save time, most feedback can be given verbally rather than in writing.

Busting some assessment myths

Many teachers mark every piece of work in their pupils' books and engage in a form of written dialogue. They mark every word and provide hugely detailed comments. This level of detail is unsustainable (if the teacher is to avoid having a nervous breakdown before Christmas) and can also be counter-productive.

Often, teachers who engage in this level of marking cite Ofsted as the reason for their practices. Certainly, it is not uncommon for school leaders to say "It's what inspectors expect to see" when defending their policies on marking.

Before we conclude this section of the book, therefore, let's bust this myth that Ofsted expect to see evidenced of detailed, frequent marking in pupils' books and favour a back-and-forth dialogue between the teacher and the pupil...

What Ofsted say about pupils' books

Ofsted are clear that they do not expect to see a particular frequency or quantity of work in pupils' books or folders. Indeed, Ofsted recognise that the amount of work in books and folders will depend on the subject being studied and the age and ability of the pupils.

Whilst Ofsted recognise that marking and feedback to pupils, both written and oral, are important aspects of assessment, they do not expect to see any specific frequency, type or volume of marking and feedback; these, they say, are for schools to decide through their assessment policy.

Marking and feedback should be consistent with a school's policy, which may cater for different subjects and different age groups of pupils in different ways, in order to be effective and efficient in promoting learning.

Whilst inspectors will consider how written and oral feedback is used to promote learning, they do not expect to see any written record of oral feedback provided to pupils by teachers.

If it is necessary for inspectors to identify marking as an area for improvement for a school, they will pay careful attention to the way recommendations are written to ensure that these do not drive unnecessary workload for teachers.

Whilst we're on the subject of Ofsted, let's bust some other popular myths…

Lesson planning

Ofsted do not require teachers to provide individual lesson plans to inspectors. Equally, Ofsted do not require teachers to provide previous lesson plans. Ofsted do not specify how planning should be set out, the length of time it should take or the amount of detail it should contain. Inspectors are interested in the effectiveness of planning rather than the form it takes.

Grading of lessons

Ofsted do not award a grade for the quality of teaching or outcomes in an individual lesson.

Lesson observations

Ofsted do not require schools to undertake a specified amount of lesson observations on a teacher, new or otherwise. Ofsted do not expect schools to provide specific details of the pay grade of individual teachers who are observed during inspection.

Evidence for inspection

Ofsted will take a range of evidence into account when making judgments, including published performance data, the school's in-year performance information and work in pupils' books and folders, including that held in electronic form. However, unnecessary or extensive collections of marked pupils' work are not required for inspection.

Ofsted does not expect performance and pupil-tracking information to be presented in a particular format. Such information should be provided to inspectors in the format that the school would ordinarily use to monitor the progress of pupils in that school.

Ofsted does not require teachers to undertake additional work or to ask pupils to undertake work specifically for the inspection.

Ofsted will usually expect to see evidence of the monitoring of teaching and learning and its link to teachers' performance management and the teachers' standards, but this should be the information that the school uses routinely and not additional evidence generated for inspection.

And finally…

Ofsted are not the enemy

An Ofsted inspection should not be feared.

Ofsted inspectors are not spies in search of your deepest, darkest secrets nor are they duplicitous interlopers intent on asking you trick questions in the hope of catching you out! They perform the necessary and important job of ensuring that schools are safe places for young people to study and that schools are institutions that provide a good quality of education. They will report on what they see and hear. They will provide an honest account of a school's strengths and weaknesses, judged against clear and widely published criteria.

It is important, therefore, that you engage with inspectors. If you don't tell inspectors what you do well, these strengths may be overlooked during the inspection process and may not therefore appear in the final report. Moreover, if you don't demonstrate that you're acutely aware of your areas for improvement and are already working hard to address each of them, then inspectors cannot be blamed for citing these issues as evidence of serious weaknesses or for suggesting that the school's self-evaluation is inaccurate and flawed because the focus is as much on the process of self-evaluation as it is on the outcomes of self-evaluation.

Part Seven

Pastoral care and SEND

Chapter Nineteen

Being an effective form tutor

A form tutor is someone who has pastoral responsibility for a cohort of pupils. In some schools they are called class mentors. Some schools have year group forms, others have 'vertical' tutor groups whereby pupils from every year come together at tutor time.

Most primary teachers are their class's form tutor and main subject teacher. Most secondary teachers are subject specialists for a range of different classes but also act as form tutors to one particular cohort of pupils.

Whether you work in a primary or a secondary school, the role of a form tutor is vital to the efficient running of the school and, more importantly, to the successful pastoral care of pupils.

A form tutor is the first point of contact to whom a pupil will turn for help and advice, although it may be necessary for the tutor to refer the pupil to their Head of Year, SENCo, and Deputy Head teacher or, through them, to an outside agency.

Top tips for tutor time

According to the National Association of Pastoral Care in Education, the form tutor should be the key person who:

- Links the pupil and home.
- Connects the pupil with school staff and with other pupils.
- Monitors academic and personal progress for the pupils in their tutor group or form.
- Provides information to other staff about their tutees.
- Co-ordinates the way the school can meet their pupils' needs.

Ideally, the tutor group and base-room will become a second home for pupils where they feel they belong.

The form tutor's role is complex but, essentially, it is to gather knowledge about each pupil, form a strong, positive relationship with each one and their home, and build the team, while modelling sound habits to support them to progress, develop and learn throughout their time at secondary school.

It is often the small things a good form tutor does to show that they care that can make a big difference to a pupil's experience of school. Ultimately, it is about caring and going the extra mile to help your pupils feel supported so that they can do their best in their studies, and to grow emotionally and socially.

It is likely that, every day, you will: take the register (perhaps twice), check uniforms, and give out notices or information to individuals or the whole tutor group.

In addition, on most days you will also find yourself:

- Talking to pupils, and listening to their discussions to pick up on any current issues.
- Dealing with various problems, including missing PE kits, late homework, detention disputes, lost locker keys, mobiles or letters from parents, and Child Protection issues.
- Keeping an eye out for anyone who seems upset, especially quiet – or indeed noisy.
- Being given letters, notes, and forms (even if they are supposed to be given in elsewhere).
- Lending out equipment such as pens and pencils (and maybe even money).
- Running, or being involved in, some kind of activity, assembly, and tutor programme.

Less often, perhaps weekly, fortnightly or termly, you might also find yourself:

- Checking that planners are being used properly and fully, and are being signed by parents/carers.
- Holding a tutor group discussion of some kind.
- Processing and recording your pupils' merits, awards, detentions, homework, problems, complaints, etc.
- Meeting to mentor or coach one or several pupils for either

academic or personal reasons.

- Dealing with a pupil's home in some way – by letter, phone call, email, text, via a note in their planner, etc.
- Discussing one or several of your pupils in depth or writing and answering emails about your pupils' progress and behaviour.
- Helping to prepare and give an assembly.
- Taking part in some kind of year/key stage/house event.
- Receiving or giving feedback to the pupil council.
- Doing something for your chosen charity.

Establishing yourself as a new tutor

Before you even meet your new tutor group, you need to be aware of the school's policies on a range of pastoral matters such as uniform, chewing, coats, entry to rooms and so on, as well as having an accurate and up-to-date list of names from your pastoral head.

You cannot possibly be expected to read every file, but it is worth asking for pointers on any looked-after children, or those with SEN or disabilities. The SENCo should have sent everyone a list of pupils, and these will probably have a brief pen portrait or at least a few notes available for staff, from the end of the summer term.

Make sure you have visited and have keys or access to your tutor base-room. This might not necessarily be your teaching room, so you will need to find out whose classroom it is and establish a positive working relationship with them and any support staff involved, such as the technician or cleaner, from the beginning.

As a new tutor you need to establish your personality and authority on the group straight away. For a new Year 7 group, this will probably entail you having to collect the pupils from the hall, (where you will have the opportunity to observe and watch out for any nervous or isolated pupils, any big personalities, etc.), and leading them to your base.

A seating plan can help to show that you are in charge of the room and it helps you to learn names quicker. The point is that you want to establish your authority and learn who they are, whilst also encouraging them to work together as a team. A plan can help you to break up any cliques that may seem unhealthy or exclusive.

Do beware of talking too much at the start. The pupils are dying to chat too, so put them in pairs to get on with the essentials together and try *asking* not *telling*, when you can.

Humour works well, as do quizzes and games to lighten the otherwise boring but vital administrative duties. For instance, having a couple of year 9 pupils visiting each tutor group in appalling uniform and giving points for each infringement noted, is more fun and memorable than droning through correct uniform lists.

Chapter Twenty

The SEND code *of* practice

The 0-25 SEND Code of Practice was introduced in 2014 and describes the principles that should be observed by all professionals working with children and young people who have special educational needs or disabilities.

These include:
- taking into account the views of children, young people and their families
- enabling children, young people and their parents to participate in decision-making
- collaborating with partners in education, health and social care to provide support
- identifying the needs of children and young people
- making high quality provision to meet the needs of children and young people
- focusing on inclusive practices and removing barriers to learning
- helping children and young people to prepare for adulthood.

All schools should have a clear approach to identifying and responding to SEN.

A pupil has SEN where their learning difficulty or disability calls for special educational provision, namely provision different from or additional to that normally available to pupils of the same age.

Ensuring that the quality teaching available to the whole class is of a consistently high standard is likely to mean that fewer pupils will require such support.

Schools should assess each pupil's current skills and levels of attainment on entry, building on information from previous settings and key stages where appropriate. At the same time, schools should consider evidence that a pupil may have a disability under the Equality Act 2010 and, if so, what reasonable adjustments may need to be made for them.

What all this means for you...

Supported by the senior leadership team, you should regularly assess the progress being made by all your pupils. These assessments should seek to identify pupils making less than expected progress given their age and individual circumstances. 'Less than expected progress' is characterised by progress which:

- is significantly slower than that of their peers starting from the same baseline
- fails to match or better the child's previous rate of progress
- fails to close the attainment gap between the child and their peers
- widens the attainment gap between the child and their peers.

It can include progress in areas other than attainment – for instance where a pupil needs to make additional progress with wider development or social needs in order to make a successful transition to adult life.

Where a pupil is making less progress than expected, the first response to such progress should be high quality teaching targeted at their areas of weakness.

Where progress continues to be less than expected, you - working with the SENCo - should help your school to assess whether the child has SEN. While informally gathering evidence (including the views of the pupil and their parents) schools should not delay in putting in place extra teaching or other rigorous interventions designed to secure better progress, where required. The pupil's response to such support can help identify their particular needs.

For some children, SEN can be identified at an early age. However, for other children and young people, difficulties become evident only as they develop.

All those who work with children and young people should be alert to emerging difficulties and respond early. In particular, parents know their children best and it is important that all professionals listen and understand when parents express concerns about their child's development. They should also listen to and address any concerns raised by children and young people themselves.

Persistent disruptive or withdrawn behaviours do not necessarily mean that a child or young person has SEN. Where there are concerns, there should be an assessment to determine whether there are any causal factors such as undiagnosed learning difficulties, difficulties with communication or mental health issues.

If it is believed that housing, family or other domestic circumstances may be contributing to the pupil's current behaviour, a multi-agency approach, supported by the use of strategies such as the Early Help Assessment, may be deemed appropriate.

In all cases, early identification and intervention can significantly reduce the use of more costly interventions at a later stage.

Professionals should also be alert to other events that can lead to learning difficulties or wider mental health difficulties, such as bullying or bereavement. Such events will not always lead to children having SEN but it can have an impact on well-being and sometimes this can be severe.

Schools should ensure they make appropriate provision for a child's short-term needs in order to prevent problems escalating. Where there are long-lasting difficulties schools should consider whether the child might have SEN.

Slow progress and low attainment do not necessarily mean that a child has SEN and should not automatically lead to a pupil being recorded as having SEN. However, they may be an indicator of a range of learning difficulties or disabilities. Equally, it should not be assumed that attainment in line with chronological age means that there is no learning difficulty or disability. For example, some children and young people may be high achieving academically, but may require additional support in communicating and interacting socially.

Some learning difficulties and disabilities occur across the range of cognitive ability and, left unaddressed, may lead to frustration, and this in turn - may manifest itself as disaffection, and emotional or behavioural difficulties.

Identifying and assessing SEN for children or young people whose first language is not English requires particular care. Schools should look carefully at all aspects of a child or young person's performance in different areas of learning and development or subjects in order to establish whether or not a lack of progress is due to limitations in their command of English or if it arises from SEN or a disability. Difficulties related solely to limitations in English as an additional language are not SEN.

When reviewing and managing special educational provision there are four broad areas of need and support which give an overview of the range of needs that should be planned for, and schools should review how well equipped they are to provide support across these areas. They are:

- Communication and interaction,
- Cognition and learning,
- Social, emotion and mental health difficulties, and
- Sensory and/or physical needs

The process

Teachers are responsible and accountable for the progress and development of the pupils in their class, including where pupils access support from teaching assistants or specialist staff.

As I say above, high quality teaching, differentiated for individual pupils, is the first step in responding to pupils who have or may have SEN.

In deciding whether to make special educational provision, the teacher and SENCo should consider all of the information gathered from within the school about the pupil's progress, alongside national data and expectations of progress. This should include high quality and accurate formative assessment, using effective tools and early assessment materials. For higher levels of need, schools should have arrangements in place to draw on more specialised assessments from external agencies and professionals.

This information gathering should include an early discussion with the pupil and their parents. These early discussions with parents should be structured in such a way that they develop a good understanding of the pupil's areas of strength and difficulty, the parents' concerns, the agreed outcomes sought for the child and the next steps.

A short note of these early discussions should be added to the pupil's record on the school information system and given to the parents. Schools should also tell parents and young people about the local authority's information, advice and support service.

Consideration of whether special educational provision is required should start with the desired outcomes, including the expected progress and attainment and the views and wishes of the pupil and their parents. This should then help determine the support that is needed and whether it can be provided by adapting the school's core offer or whether something different or additional is required.

Where a pupil is identified as having SEN, schools should take action to remove barriers to learning and put effective special educational provision in place. This SEN support should take the form of a four-part cycle (assess, plan, do, review) through which earlier decisions and actions are revisited, refined and revised with a growing understanding of the pupil's needs and of what supports the pupil in making good progress and securing good outcomes. This is known as the graduated approach. It draws on more detailed approaches, more frequent review and more specialist expertise in successive cycles in order to match interventions to the special educational needs of children and young people.

Parents should be fully aware of the planned support and interventions and, where appropriate, plans should seek parental involvement to reinforce or contribute to progress at home. Parents should also be involved in the various reviews of the support that is provided to their child and have clear information about the impact of this support and any interventions, enabling them to be involved in planning next steps.

Chapter Twenty-One

The SEND code *in* practice

In Chapter Twenty we looked at the SEND code of practice. Now let's turn that 'code of practice' into a 'code in practice'…

First of all, it's important to note that supporting pupils with SEN is not a matter for a teacher or their school alone; rather, they should involve the pupil and their parents, and external specialists where necessary.

Involving specialists

Where a pupil continues to make less than expected progress, despite evidence-based support and interventions that are matched to the pupil's areas of need, the school should consider involving specialists, including those secured by the school itself or from outside agencies. This could include, for example, speech and language therapists, specialist teachers for the hearing or vision impaired, occupational therapists or physiotherapists.

Schools may involve specialists at any point to advise them on early identification of SEN and effective support and interventions. The pupil's parents should always be involved in any decision to involve specialists. The involvement of specialists and what was discussed or agreed should be recorded and shared with the parents and teaching staff supporting the child in the same way as other SEN support.

The SENCo and class teacher, together with the specialists, and involving the pupil's parents, should consider a range of evidence-based and effective teaching approaches, appropriate equipment, strategies and interventions in order to support the child's progress. They should agree the outcomes to be achieved through the support, including a date by which progress will be reviewed.

Involving parents and pupils in planning and reviewing progress

Schools must provide an annual report for parents on their child's progress. Most schools will want to go beyond this and provide regular reports for parents on how their child is progressing. Where a pupil is receiving SEN support, schools should talk to parents regularly to set clear outcomes and review progress towards them, discuss the activities and support that will help achieve them, and identify the responsibilities of the parent, the pupil and the school.

Schools should meet parents at least three times each year. The views of the pupil should be included in these discussions. This could be through involving the pupil in all or part of the discussion itself, or gathering their views as part of the preparation.

A record of the outcomes, action and support agreed through the discussion should be kept and shared with all the appropriate school staff. This record should be given to the pupil's parents. The school's management information system should be updated as appropriate.

Support before Year 9

When a child is very young, or SEN is first identified, families need to know that the great majority of children and young people with SEN or disabilities, with the right support, can find work, be supported to live independently, and participate in their community.

Health workers, social workers, early years providers and schools should encourage these ambitions right from the start. They should seek to understand the interests, strengths and motivations of children and young people and use this as a basis for planning support around them. Schools should support children and young people so that they are included in social groups and develop friendships. This is particularly important when children and young people are transferring from one phase of education to another (for example, from nursery to primary school). Maintained schools must ensure that, subject to certain conditions, pupils with SEN engage in the activities of the school together with those who do not have SEN, and are encouraged to participate fully in the life of the school and in any wider community activity.

Support from Year 9 onwards

High aspirations about employment, independent living and community participation should be developed through the curriculum and extra-curricular provision. Schools should seek partnerships with employment services, businesses, housing agencies, disability organisations and arts and sports groups, to help children understand what is available to them as they get older, and what it is possible for them to achieve. It can be particularly powerful to meet disabled adults who are successful in their work or who have made a significant contribution to their community.

Preparing for adulthood should form part of the planning for all children and young people with SEN and disabilities, right from the earliest years. However, for teenagers, preparation for adult life needs to be a more explicit element of their planning and support. Discussions about their future should focus on what they want to achieve and the best way to support them to achieve.

For children and young people with EHC plans, local authorities must ensure that the EHC plan review at Year 9, and every review thereafter, includes a focus on preparing for adulthood. The SEND Code of Practice provides further information about what should be included in preparing for adulthood reviews (see Chapter 8, Preparing for adulthood from the earliest years).

After compulsory school age (the end of the academic year in which they turn 16) the right to make requests and decisions under the Children and Families Act 2014 applies to young people directly, rather than to their parents. Parents, or other family members, can continue to support young people in making decisions, or act on their behalf, provided that the young person is happy for them to do so, and it is likely that parents will remain closely involved in the great majority of cases. This is particularly important for young people under 18 and schools would normally involve parents or family members where they have concerns about a young person's behaviour or welfare. They should also continue to involve parents or family members in discussions about the young person's studies where that is their usual policy.

The fact that the Children and Families Act 2014 gives rights directly to young people from the end of compulsory school age does not necessitate any change to a school's safeguarding or welfare policy.

Supporting pupils with SEND in the classroom

Young people with SEND are not the sole domain of the school's SENCo. With one in five children identified as having SEND, the reality for many teachers is that around five to seven pupils in each class may have SEND and so every teacher needs to take responsibility.

Providing effective support for all pupils in a school is about strengthening collaboration but still maintaining responsibility for the pupils and taking an adaptive approach to teaching.

What all this means for you...

You should use additional resources to address targeted support for pupils and focus on better understanding the outcomes of that support. In particular, you should ask:

- What progress has been made towards agreed outcomes?
- How has the additional support enabled the pupil to achieve this as independently as possible?
- What is the pupil's view on this?
- What is the view of the teaching assistant, other teachers, and (maybe) the pupil's peers?

This reflective, adaptive approach is integral to good SEND practice, and something which should be nurtured to become standard practice within the classroom.

Always remember that no two pupils are the same, even if their needs are identified as belonging to the same area of need.

As we learnt in the previous chapter, the SEND Code of Practice identifies four broad areas of need:
1. Communication and interaction,
2. Cognition and learning,
3. Social, mental and emotional health, and

4.   Sensory and/or physical needs.

However, it is important to remember that SEND is a hugely broad term, covering children with needs ranging from the complex and physical, to mild learning difficulties. Part of the challenge is being able to adapt your classroom teaching to ensure that all children will be able to engage and learn.

A core part of the graduated approach to SEND is, as I said in Chapter Twenty, to 'assess, plan, do, and review'. Therefore, you need to constantly assess a pupil's needs before planning how to address those needs and then implement this plan.

This is a continuous cycle that should be constantly under review with agreed dates and times to appraise outcomes regularly (every two to six weeks is good practice) so that you and the SENCo can act swiftly to tweak and adapt any arrangements accordingly.

Ultimately, the best advice of all is to get to know your pupils, their individual needs and the ways in which you can help them to get the most out of school. You must continue to have high expectations of all children and present the level of challenge they need.

Part Eight

Safeguarding

Chapter Twenty-Two

Child protection

Let's start with the big question: What is child protection?

Ofsted adopts the definition of child protection that's used in the Children Act 2004 and in the Department for Education guidance document, 'Working together to safeguard children', which focuses on safeguarding and promoting children's and learners' welfare. For the purposes of this book and to achieve consistency and clarity, I will adopt the same definition which can be summarised as:

- protecting children and learners from maltreatment
- preventing impairment of children's and learners' health or development
- ensuring that children and learners are growing up in circumstances consistent with the provision of safe and effective care
- undertaking that role so as to enable those children and learners to have optimum life chances and to enter adulthood successfully.

The DfE guidance, 'Safeguarding children and safer recruitment in education', meanwhile, makes it clear that schools must provide a safe environment and take action to identify and protect any children or young people who are at risk of significant harm.

Schools are required to prevent unsuitable people from working with children and young people; to promote safe practice and challenge unsafe practice; to ensure that staff receive the necessary training for their roles; and to work in partnership with other agencies providing services for children and young people.

Here are some of the key features of effective safeguarding practice:

- High-quality leadership and management that makes safeguarding a priority across all aspects of a school's work

- Having stringent vetting procedures in place for staff and other adults
- Having rigorous safeguarding policies and procedures in place, written in plain English, compliant with statutory requirements and updated regularly; in particular, clear and coherent child protection policies
- Ensuring child protection arrangements are accessible to everyone, so that pupils and families, as well as adults in the school, know who they can talk to if they are worried
- Ensuring there are excellent communication systems in place with up-to-date information that can be accessed and shared by those who need it
- Giving a high priority to training in safeguarding, generally going beyond basic requirements, extending expertise widely and building internal capacity
- Putting in place robust arrangements for site security which are understood and applied by staff and pupils
- Having a curriculum that is flexible, relevant and engages pupils' interest; that is used to promote safeguarding, not least through teaching pupils how to stay safe, how to protect themselves from harm and how to take responsibility for their own and others' safety
- Securing courteous and responsible behaviour by pupils, enabling everyone to feel secure and well-protected
- Having well-thought-out and workable day-to-day arrangements to protect and promote pupils' health and safety
- Ensuring the rigorous monitoring of absence, with timely and appropriate follow-up, to ensure that pupils attend regularly
- Taking risk assessments seriously and using them to good effect in promoting safety.

Teachers' child protection duties

A number of statutory provisions place responsibilities for child protection upon local authorities (LAs), schools, academies and colleges. Under the Children Act 1989, for example, local authorities, schools (including academies) and colleges have a duty to assist local authority social services departments acting on behalf of children in need or enquiring into allegations of child abuse.

Education bodies have a statutory duty to carry out their functions with a view to safeguarding and promoting the welfare of children under the Education Act 2002 and accompanying regulations. This includes taking steps to protect children who are at risk of significant harm. Harm is defined as ill treatment or the impairment of a child's physical or mental health or of their physical, intellectual, emotional, social or behavioural development.

The duty applies to local authorities, governing bodies of community, foundation, voluntary aided, voluntary controlled, special and maintained nursery schools and FE colleges, and the proprietors of independent schools, including academies.

Besides these statutory duties, schools (including academies) and colleges have a pastoral responsibility towards their pupils.

What all this means for you…

Your individual responsibilities depend upon your role in relation to child protection in your school.

The DfE issued guidance to maintained and independent schools (including academies), and colleges, called 'Dealing with Allegations of Abuse Against Teachers and other Staff' which sets out how individuals and organisations should work together to safeguard and promote the welfare of children.

Briefly, it says that:
- Teachers should be familiar with the procedures in their school, academy or college for dealing with suspected child abuse. Concern or suspicions should be reported.
- Each school, academy or college should have a designated member of staff responsible for child protection matters. The 'designated person' will usually be a teacher and he or she must undertake regular training on child protection and inter-agency work.
- All other staff, including supply teachers and fixed-term teachers, should receive appropriate training on child protection issues.
- Child abuse is widely defined, but may include physical

abuse; emotional abuse (which is the persistent emotional maltreatment of a child such as to cause severe and persistent adverse effects on the child's emotional development); sexual abuse (which involves forcing or enticing a child or young person to take part in sexual activities, including prostitution); and neglect (which is the persistent failure to meet a child's basic physical and/or psychological needs, and is likely to result in the serious impairment of the child's health or development).

- Teachers are not responsible for investigating suspected abuse but should know to whom they should report any concerns. It is the responsibility of the designated teachers to discuss cases with, or refer cases to, the investigating agencies, which are social services departments and the police.
- All schools, academies and colleges should have procedures, of which all staff should be aware, for handling suspected cases of abuse of pupils or by pupils. The school, academy or college child protection policy should also be made known to parents.
- Each school, academy and college should also have procedures for dealing with allegations of physical or sexual abuse which have been made against members of staff.

Child protection in practice

In practical terms, it is important to know that every school will have a designated child protection lead – usually, but not always, the senior leader (deputy head teacher) in charge of pastoral care. One of your tasks when you start is to find out who this person is. If ever a child discloses a child protection matter to you, your first action must be to inform the child protection lead.

Your school will also have its own safeguarding policy. Your second task, therefore, is to locate and read this policy so you understand precisely what is expected of you.

You will, as a matter of course, receive safeguarding training from your school. You are not alone in dealing with child protection matters and will be fully supported at all times by your colleagues and by your professional association. If ever in doubt, ask.

So far we've looked at your legal duties in relation to child protection and safeguarding. In Chapter Twenty-Three we will consider what other legal duties you adopt when you become a teacher.

M J Bromley

Chapter Twenty-Three

Your legal duties

Teachers have a number of other legal duties such as their duty of care towards pupils.

Teachers are required to do all that is reasonable to protect the health, safety and welfare of pupils. Their legal responsibilities derive from three sources:
1.   The common law duty of care;
2.   The statutory duty of care; and
3.   The duty arising from the contract of employment.

1. The common law duty of care

Teachers have a duty of care to pupils which derives from the 'common law'. The 'common law' is law developed through decisions of the Court as opposed to law which has been determined by Parliament and set down in statute.

Traditionally, the term 'in loco parentis' was used to describe the duty of care that a teacher has towards a pupil, to the effect that a teacher has a duty to take the same reasonable care of the pupil that a parent would take in those circumstances. 'In loco parentis' originally embodied the nineteenth century common law principle that a teacher's authority was delegated by a parent so far as it was necessary for the welfare of the child. A court held, in 1893, that "the schoolmaster is bound to take such care of his pupils as a careful father would".

During the 1950s and 1960s, case law was developed further by the courts. In 1955, it was held that "a balance must be struck between the meticulous supervision of children every moment of the day and the desirable object of encouraging sturdy independence as they grow up".

Teachers' professionalism was recognised by the courts in 1962, where the 'standard of care' expected of a teacher was held to be that of a person exhibiting the responsible mental qualities of a prudent parent in the circumstances of school, rather than home life. The current standard of care expected of a teacher is that of a reasonable person in the circumstances of a class teacher. It has been recognised that a teacher's duty of care to individual pupils is influenced by, for example, the subject or activity being taught, the age of the children, the available resources and the size of the class.

Further, it is clear from case law that the standard of care expected is the application of the ordinary skills of a competent professional, the skill and care of a reasonable teacher.

If it can be shown that a professional acted in accordance with the views of a reputable body of opinion within their profession, the duty of care will have been satisfied, even though others may disagree.

A breach of the duty of care by a teacher could amount to common law negligence.

A teacher's employer could be liable for the payment of damages in compensation to a pupil who is injured as a result of negligence.

Whether teachers are found negligent in the event of accidents will be influenced by whether the incident that occurred could have reasonably been foreseen. If teachers take all reasonable steps to ensure the safety of their pupils, it is unlikely that a teacher will be held to be negligent in the event of an unforeseen accident.

Negligence could also arise if there is a serious failure to prevent harm to a child arising from, for example, pupil bullying. If negligence arises in these circumstances, it is more likely to be a collective failing rather than the responsibility of one individual.

A teacher's duty of care will depend upon what is reasonable and what can be expected of a competent professional acting within the constraints of the circumstances

As long as teachers apply their professional judgment, training and experience to situations in a reasonable manner, seeking to promote the best interests of the pupils in their care, their obligations will have been met.

2. The statutory duty of care

Teachers are also responsible under the Children Act which places statutory duties upon those who care for children.

The Children Act 1989 Section 3 (5) defines the duty of care to the effect that a person with care of a child may do all that is reasonable in the circumstances for the purposes of safeguarding or promoting the welfare of the child.

When issues arise concerning safeguarding or promoting the welfare of children, teachers should take into account the ascertainable needs and wishes of the children as individuals, considered in the light of their ages, understanding and any risk of harm.

3. The contractual duty of care

A duty of care also arises from a teacher's contract of employment, the terms of which will depend on the type of school in which the teacher works.

The School Teachers' Pay and Conditions Document (STPCD) expressly defines the contractual duties in England and Wales upon all teachers employed in maintained schools. It also applies to teachers in independent schools (including academies) where the STPCD has been incorporated into their contracts. The document takes effect by statutory order and is revised annually, the new provisions becoming effective in September of each year.

Relevant provisions from the list of contractual duties include:
- planning and teaching lessons to the classes they are assigned to teach within the context of the school's plans, curriculum and schemes of work;
- assessing, monitoring, recording and reporting on the learning needs, progress and achievements of assigned pupils;
- promoting the safety and well-being of pupils and maintaining good order and discipline among pupils; and
- participating in arrangements for their own further training and professional development, and, where appropriate, that of

other teachers and support staff, including induction.

Chapter Twenty-Four

Health and safety

The main responsibility under the Health and Safety at Work Act (HSWA) 1974 rests with employers, who have to take reasonable care for the health and safety of their employees and others on their premises.

Employers are required to organise, control, monitor and review how health and safety measures are managed. They must assess risks, record their assessments of risks and inform employees of safety procedures. Schools (including academies) and colleges should have written health and safety policies in place, of which all employees, including teachers, should be informed. Furthermore, Section 2 of the HSWA requires employers to consult with safety representatives on health and safety matters.

The duty on employers includes taking reasonable care for both the physical and mental health of their employees. This means that employers should assess the risks to teachers of excessive workload, pupil behaviour and the conduct of other staff.

What all this means for you….

You have a duty under the Health and Safety at Work Act to take reasonable care for your own health and safety and that of others who may be affected by your acts or omissions at work.

Specifically, you have a duty to take reasonable care of both your own and your pupils' health and safety at school.

In practice, this means that you should comply with any school and/or local authority guidance on health and safety issues and make sure that you are familiar with any such guidance.

You should act with reasonable care at all times and apply good sense to everything you do, including not taking any unnecessary risk or doing anything that is potentially dangerous.

It is unlawful to interfere with, or misuse (either intentionally or recklessly) anything which has been provided for the purposes of health and safety. For example, do not prop open fire doors, misuse fire extinguishers or first aid kits, or block fire exits.

You also have a duty to report any hazards and potentially dangerous incidents at work and you should familiarise yourself with any recording system in the school, such as the accident log book.

It can be important to report what might seem to be minor matters requiring cleaning up or minor repair. Seemingly minor matters can cause serious accidents. For example, wet patches or rubbish on the floor could cause slips, trips or falls.

Out-of-school activities

Understanding the duty of care can be particularly significant when a teacher is engaged in leading or assisting with activities off the school site, such as educational visits, school outings or field trips.

The legal liability of an individual teacher or head teacher for an injury which is sustained by a pupil on a school journey or excursion depends on whether or not the injury to the pupil is a direct result of some negligence or breach of the duty of care on the part of their teacher or head teacher. There is no legal liability for any injury sustained by pupils unless there is proven negligence.

The standard of care required of teachers is that which, from an objective point of view, can reasonably be expected from teachers generally applying skill and awareness of children's problems, needs and susceptibilities. The law expects that a teacher will do that which a parent with care and concern for the safety and welfare of his or her own child would do, bearing in mind that being responsible for up to twenty pupils is very different from looking after a family.

The legal duty of care expected of an individual teacher is that which a caring teaching profession would expect of itself. In practice, this means that teachers must provide supervision of the pupils throughout school journeys or visits according to professional standards and common sense.

Reasonable steps must be taken to avoid exposing pupils to dangers which are foreseeable and beyond those with which the particular pupils can reasonably be expected to cope. This does not imply constant 24-hour direct supervision. The need for direct supervision has to be judged by reference to the risks involved in the activity being undertaken. It may not always be sufficient to give instructions to pupils.

The possibility that there may be challenging behaviour has to be taken into account, together with the risk the pupils may encounter if they disobey instructions. Equally, teachers may take account of the ages and levels of personal responsibility of their pupils.

Teachers have responsibility for pupils in their care but qualified instructors giving guidance to pupils will be responsible for their relevant area of expertise. If teachers are concerned about the ability of any of their pupils to undertake any particular activity safely, those pupils should, if necessary, be withdrawn from the activity.

Teachers should not participate in journeys or visits which they believe are not being adequately prepared and organised. Any concerns should be raised with the head teacher and, if the response is unsatisfactory or concerns remain, with the teacher's professional association.

Where journeys are organised within schools, responsibility for establishing that proper preparation has been made and that proper supervision will be provided lies ultimately with the head teacher. Head teachers may delegate this function to an educational visits coordinator (EVC).

Satisfying the duty of care absolves teachers from legal liability. Sometimes accidents occur as a result of the fault of persons with no organising or supervising responsibility for the journey. Some events are accidents, not reasonably foreseeable and not the result of anyone's negligence. Liability goes with fault. In the case of a pure accident, no one bears liability. 'No-fault' insurance covers this eventuality.

Employers have 'vicarious liability' for the negligence of their employees at work. This means broadly that the employer takes responsibility if employees do not properly fulfil their health and safety obligations at work. Accidents involving pupils where negligence is alleged on the part of teachers may give rise to legal claims. If the teachers involved were working in the course of their employment at the time an incident occurred, such legal claims will most likely be made against employers. The employer might be the local authority or, in the case of a foundation school, voluntary aided school, Sixth Form College, independent school, academy or trust school, the governing body and/or board of trustees.

In 2011 the Department for Education withdrew its longstanding guidance on school trips called 'Health and Safety of Pupils on Educational Visits' (known as HASPEV), and replaced it with an eight-page summary of the law relating to health and safety both in schools generally and on school visits specifically. Some elements of the guidance have proven particularly controversial, such as the statement that "teachers should assume they only need to carry out a written risk assessment in exceptional circumstances." It's always best to read your school's policies and to seek guidance from your head teacher, head of department, and/or EVC.

Physical contact with pupils

Contrary to popular opinion, it is not illegal to touch a pupil. There are occasions when physical contact, other than reasonable force, with a pupil is proper and necessary. However, you should always seek to avoid physical contact with pupils.

Examples of where touching a pupil might be proper or necessary include:
- Holding the hand of the child at the front/back of the line when going to assembly or when walking together around the school;
- When comforting a distressed pupil;
- When a pupil is being congratulated or praised;
- To demonstrate how to use a musical instrument;

- To demonstrate exercises or techniques during PE lessons or sports coaching; and
- To give first aid.

Again, and I cannot emphasise this enough, you should avoid any situations in which you are likely to have to make physical contact with pupils, no matter how innocent it is. You should certainly not make physical contact with a pupil when you and they are alone.

Teachers' powers to use reasonable force to restrain

As I've said, you should always avoid physical contact with pupils and remove yourself from situations in which you will have to use reasonable force. Defer to senior colleagues if necessary. If in doubt, do not intervene – ask for help. However…

If it is unavoidable, the law states that teachers are generally permitted the use of reasonable force to prevent pupils from hurting themselves or others, from damaging property, or from causing disorder.

The DfE guidance on the 'Use of Reasonable Restraint' provides that teachers can use reasonable force:
- to remove disruptive children from the classroom where they have refused to follow an instruction to do so
- to prevent a pupil behaving in a way that disrupts a school event or a school trip or visit
- to prevent a pupil leaving the classroom where allowing the pupil to leave would risk their safety or lead to behaviour that disrupts the behaviour of others
- to prevent a pupil from attacking a member of staff or another pupil, or to stop a fight in the playground.

The statutory provisions can apply when a teacher or other authorised person is:
- on the premises of the school (or academy); or
- elsewhere at a time when, as a member of school staff (or academy staff), he or she has lawful control or charge of the pupil concerned, for example, on an out-of-school activity.

It should be noted that the use of any degree of force is unlawful if the particular circumstances do not warrant it. The degree of force should be in proportion to the circumstances and the seriousness of the behaviour or consequences it is intended to prevent. The level and duration of the force used should be the minimum necessary to achieve the desired result, such as to restore safety.

It is always unlawful to use force as a form of punishment or discipline.

It is impossible to describe definitively when it is reasonable to use force and how much may be used, beyond stating that this will depend on the circumstances of the case. Relevant considerations as to whether it might be reasonable to use force and the degree of force to be used could include, for example, the age and strength of the child. In some circumstances it will, of course, be inadvisable for a teacher to intervene without help, such as where a number of pupils are involved, where the pupil is older and physically mature, and where the teacher might be at risk of injury.

It is relevant that failure to respond in circumstances which merit it can be as serious as overreacting…

In some circumstances, for example, it is not the safer option for a teacher to do nothing or to take very limited action, when to take action could restore safety. This action may involve swiftly alerting a third party.

So far as a teacher's duty of care is concerned, a failure to act can be significant if there is a subsequent claim for negligence. This will depend on the circumstances of the case and teachers would not be expected to intervene to restore safety at the expense of their own personal safety.

Recording and Reporting Incidents

Incidents of restraint should be logged in a record book provided for this purpose and monitored by a senior staff member. The record should be contemporaneous and detailed, as this will help in the event of any later investigation or complaint. Similarly, it is advisable to inform parents of any recorded incident.

Teachers should be familiar with their school's behaviour policy. Schools are legally required to have such policies in place. There is no legal requirement to have a policy on the use of force, but DfE guidance recommends that, as a matter of good practice, schools should set out in their behaviour policy the circumstances in which force might be used. This is likely, according to DfE guidance, to reduce the likelihood of complaints being made when force has been used properly.

Part Nine

Professional development

Chapter Twenty-Five

Making the most of INSET

Continuing Professional Development (CPD) is the term used to describe the learning activities in which teachers – and indeed other professionals – engage in order to develop and enhance their abilities.

CPD enables learning to become conscious and proactive, rather than passive and reactive.

Most of the formal CPD you will receive in school will take the form of:

- *INSET days* – these are days in the school year that are closed to pupils but that you attend school as usual for training, sometimes involving outside speakers
- *Twilight* – this is a form of INSET that takes place after the school day has finished. Some schools 'disaggregate' some of their INSET days so that you get extra holidays but attend several evening training sessions instead
- *Induction* – this is a programme of support, including access to specialised twilight training, day courses, and mentor meetings, offered to you throughout your first year of teaching and aimed at helping you settle in at your new school and become familiar with its policies and practices
- *NQT year* – this is an induction programme specially designed for newly qualified teachers who have passed their teacher-training qualification but need to complete a probation year in order to be awarded qualified teacher status (QTS).

As well as this formal CPD, there will be plenty of opportunities for you to engage in more informal, personalised professional development...

In order to make the most of opportunities for CPD, you should fully utilise five common forms of support: lesson observations and co-construction; TeachMeets and training courses; research, books, blogs and social media; coaching and mentoring; and video and lesson study.

In this chapter we'll consider lesson observations and co-construction, TeachMeets and training courses, and research, books, blogs and social media. And then, in Chapter Twenty-Six, we'll look at coaching and mentoring, and in Chapter Twenty-Seven we'll look at the use of video and lesson study…

Lesson observations and co-construction

Lesson observations

You school is likely to operate an 'open door' policy whereby it is common for colleagues to walk into each other's classrooms at any time to observe each other teaching. This is not something to be feared – no formal judgments are being made about the abilities of the teacher. It is a rich form of CPD whereby both colleagues learn valuable lessons that help them improve their practice.

As such, a key feature of your first year will be 'open door' observations. Prior to any informal observations like this, talk to the colleague who will be observing you to agree the parameters. For example, highlight specific pupils or groups of pupils and, if the type of observation permits it, ask them to focus on reactions from, or interactions with, these pupils.

Describe particular approaches you'll be using and the reactions/behaviours you hope these will solicit from pupils. Ask the observer to bear this in mind when observing the lesson. In the subsequent feedback session, relate all comments or discussions around your practice to the impact on these particular pupils. It will help to be specific.

Co-construction

A great way to develop your teaching practice is to plan lessons alongside other colleagues. Many departments do this as a matter of course because they have a collegiate culture, they pool resources such as schemes of work with a view to sharing best practice and reducing each other's workloads.

Where possible, plan a lesson that a colleague can come and observe, being sure to focus on outcomes for pupils rather than on perfecting certain teaching techniques.

Co-planning lessons is one of the four pillars of effective CPD that Judith Litttle, an American educational researcher at the University of California, Berkeley, says the most successful schools have in common…

The four pillars of CPD

1. Teachers talk about learning.

INSET is dedicated to talking about lessons, about pupils, and about teaching and learning in general. INSET is never used to discuss administrative matters, this is done by other means such as email, memos, a chat in the corridor, etc.

2. Teachers observe each other.

CPD provides opportunities for teachers to engage in a planned programme of peer observations and feedback. Peer observations are then followed by constructive, focused discussions about how teachers can improve and about how teachers can share good practice and celebrate each other's skills and talents.

Peer-observations and more informal 'walk throughs' (or 'learning walks') allow colleagues to take genuine snapshots of what happens every day, snapshots which can provide helpful suggestions for improvement as well as recognise and then reward genuine success.

3. Teachers plan together.

Judith Little talks of teachers writing lesson plans together, teaching the same lessons, and then discussing them. Many schools do not require detailed lesson plans - and Ofsted no longer requires them - so perhaps 'teachers plan together' could be interpreted as teachers talking to each other about their medium- and long-term planning, and about their marking and pupils' work.

CPD might involves teachers routinely scrutinising each other's work and moderating each other's assessments, perhaps engaging in a process of peer review of each other's mark-books and pupils' work. Where it is logistically possible, CPD could also include the use of 'lesson study' whereby colleagues plan and teach the same lesson and carry out an evaluation of its strengths and weaknesses.

4. Teachers teach each other.

INSET events and meetings are transformed into professional learning communities which provide opportunities for teachers to share practice and comment on what they've tried and what worked and what didn't. PLCs are staff-led, collaborative enterprises not opportunities for SLT to stand and deliver.

What all this means for you...

One logical conclusion of Little's four pillars is that CPD performs two functions: innovation and mastery. In other words, CPD is not just about learning new ways of working – or *CPD for innovation* – although this is undoubtedly important. It is also about helping you to get better at something you already do – or *CPD for mastery*. CPD for mastery is about recognising what works well now and what should therefore be embedded, added to, and shared.

Sometimes, CPD should be about you and your colleagues working together in pairs or small groups in order to improve on the things you already do.

TeachMeets and training courses

TeachMeets are informal meetings of teachers in which attendees share mini-presentations about their ideas for teaching. They are a great way to meet people, get stimulating teaching ideas, and share your own ideas and strategies. They take place across the country and throughout the year. Your own school may hold one. They are advertised widely including on Twitter and other social media. There is no obligation to participate so don't be afraid to go along to soak up some inspiring ideas from others.

Throughout the year you will also be able to participate in a variety of training sessions, both in school and externally. Rather than attempting to put into practice every new strategy you encounter at once, you should introduce one or two tweaks and make directed efforts to sustain and develop these. Make a note to yourself to follow up on certain training sessions at regular intervals: say, after one week, one month, three months and six months. At these regular intervals, go back to your notes and review what impact the new knowledge is having on your teaching and on pupil progress.

Research, books, blogs and social media

There is no shortage of books on teaching and learning to inform and inspire you, and your school library - or local library - is likely to have a heathy stack for you to dip in to. As well as books, you may wish to subscribe to a research newsletter in order to access regular evidence-based academic information. Many are free of charge or offer evaluation articles for free.

When looking at research, try to find summaries (or "meta-analyses") rather than reading full, single papers. This will ensure that you get a more rounded view that covers a full range of opinion.

Social media is another great source of research and opinion. Twitter, in particular, can be a useful tool for teachers. Following the Twitter accounts of some of the top bloggers and thinkers (see, for example, *@mj_bromley*!) can really stimulate you to reflect on your own practice.

You don't have to contribute to the debate, although for many teachers engaging in the discussion can help clarify their own ideas.

To begin with, simply find a few key people to follow and start reading and thinking. Subscribe to some teacher blogs, too, and sign up to emails from The Guardian Teacher Network, SecEd, TES, and other education publications.

In the next chapter we will look at the part coaching and mentoring can play in your professional development…

Chapter Twenty-Six

Coaching and mentoring

As a new teacher, the member of staff designated to mentor you will be a rich source of support and learning. Your mentor will act as a professional model and should support you to develop your professional skills.

Remember that the relationship is not designed to merely judge you; instead, it should be a safe relationship within which you are able to discuss your practice openly and frankly.

Use conversations with your mentor to be honest about the things you think you are doing well as well as the things you feel you need to develop further. Do not be afraid to ask for their support and advice.

As with observations, try to keep a particular pupil at the centre of your conversations.

As well as having a mentor, you may have - or may be able to request - a coach. The two roles are very different. Let me explain...

Coaching usually involves focused professional dialogue designed to aid you in developing specific skills to enhance your teaching repertoire. It often supports experimentation with new classroom strategies. Coaches are not normally in positions of line management. Coaching for enhancing teaching and learning is not normally explicitly linked to a career transition. The focus of the coaching is usually selected by you and the process provides opportunities for reflection and problem solving for both you and the coach.

Mentoring, meanwhile, usually takes place at significant career events, such as to support your induction or when you take on a new professional role. It has an element of 'gatekeeping' and your mentor is almost always someone more senior in the organisation. There is often an organisational motive for the process; for example, succession planning. In some cases there is a requirement that the mentor provides documentary evidence of the mentoring process and its outcomes; for example, demonstrating that you have met certain competences.

The purpose of coaching is to bring out the best in you by helping you to unlock your potential. Coaching is about teasing out answers from you through questioning and through challenging your perceptions and understanding. Coaching is about encouraging you to explore a situation you've recently experienced (or a situation you are about to experience) from a range of different angles and perspectives so that you might learn from those experiences and so that you might find your own solutions. A coach does not need to know more about a situation than you do; indeed, no expert knowledge is needed and the best coaches are often peers.

Let's look at the ten principles of coaching according to CUREE's National Framework for coaching...

Ten coaching principles

1. A learning conversation: structured professional dialogue, rooted in evidence from the professional learner's practice, which articulates existing beliefs and practices to enable reflection on them.
2. Setting challenging and personal goals: identifying goals that build on what learners know and can do already, but could not yet achieve alone, whilst attending to both school and individual priorities.
3. A thoughtful relationship: developing trust, attending respectfully and with sensitivity to the powerful emotions involved in deep professional learning.
4. Understanding why different approaches work: developing understanding of the theory that underpins new practice so it can be interpreted and adapted for different contexts.
5. A learning agreement: establishing confidence about the boundaries of the relationship by agreeing and upholding ground rules that address imbalances in power and accountability.

6.   Acknowledging the benefits to the mentors and coaches: recognising and making use of the professional learning that mentors and coaches gain from the opportunity to mentor or coach.

7.   Combining support from fellow professional learners and specialists: collaborating with colleagues to sustain commitment to learning and relate new approaches to everyday practice; seeking out specialist expertise to extend skills and knowledge and to model good practice.

8.   Experimenting and observing: creating a learning environment that supports risk-taking and innovation and encourages professional learners to seek out direct evidence from practice.

9.   Growing self-direction: an evolving process in which the learner takes increasing responsibility for their professional development as skills, knowledge and self-awareness increase.

10.   Using resources effectively: making and using time and other resources creatively to protect and sustain learning, action and reflection on a day-to-day basis.

Five coaching skills

As well as obeying these ten principles, the most effective coaching tends to be grounded in these five key skills:

1.   Establishing rapport and trust
2.   Listening for meaning
3.   Questioning for understanding
4.   Prompting action, reflection and learning
5.   Developing confidence and celebrating success

A coach must: establish high levels of trust; be consistent over time; offer genuine respect; be honest, frank and open; and challenge without threat.

A coach must not: give answers or advice; make judgments; offer counselling; create dependency; impose agendas or initiatives; and confirm long-held prejudices.

What all this means for you...

The benefits of coaching and mentoring are perhaps obvious: you will become more motivated and your confidence will grow; your knowledge and skills will be enhanced and your experience will be enlarged – because you will learn more about yourself and more about your job as a result of the process. What's more, you will develop a strong professional relationship with a colleague and have a sounding board against which to bounce ideas, concerns and theories.

In the next chapter we will continue our exploration of continuing professional development by looking at the role of video and at the process of lesson study...

Chapter Twenty-Seven

Video and lesson study

Video

Filming yourself can unlock huge potential for professional learning.

It may sound daunting, but a video camera or other recording device (such as a tablet or smart phone) positioned at the back of the class, filming material for you to watch later, can help you learn a lot about your practice. But do not fear: this form of CPD is uncommon and is unlikely to happen without your prior agreement. In fact, it doesn't happen at all in many schools – perhaps you could be a trailblazer?

If you do decide to give it a go, video works even better if you find a trusted colleague and agree to pair up to work with each other. A good tip is to focus on the way pupils are learning and reacting, rather than being too preoccupied by how you look on video! It also works best if you have a very clear focus for each lesson you film and draft some key questions to answer when you watch and analyse the video.

Lesson study

Lesson study is a process of action research which involves colleagues planning, teaching, observing and analysing a lesson together.

Here's the lesson study process in summary form:
1. Three or four teachers plan a lesson together
2. The activity they plan addresses a specific learning outcome
3. Teachers predict how pupils will react to the activity
4. A case study of three pupils is selected, perhaps based on prior assessment
5. The lesson is taught and observed, particular attention is given to the case study pupils
6. An assessment is carried out and pupils are interviewed

7.   The teachers reflect on their findings (in relation to their predictions) and plan their response

The lesson study process in more detail...

Firstly, perhaps with the help of a coach or subject leader, a group of three or four teachers (a triad or quad) identifies a research question – using data collected from their assessments of pupils – such as 'What impact will peer-assessment have on the quality of the written work of Year 11 grade 4/5 borderline pupils in the response to non-fiction unit of GCSE English?'

The research question, like the one above, should be focused and specific; it should identify the learning outcome which the lesson study seeks to improve (e.g. the quality of written work); the pupils who will be involved in the study (Year 11 grade 4/5 borderline English pupils); the teaching and learning strategy which is to be tested (peer-assessment); and the unit or scheme of work (GCSE English 'response to non-fiction').

It's also important at the planning stage that the teachers in the triad identify the means by which they will evaluate the impact of their project. For example, the triad might want to create a test for pupils to complete before and after the project and agree a set of interview questions for pupils to answer.

Secondly, the lesson is planned collaboratively and is then taught and observed. The observation is focused on the case study pupils' learning and progress; it is not a general observation of quality of teaching and learning. The process may be repeated and the activities refined over time. Not all the lessons in the study need to be observed.

One alternative to 'live' peer-observation – and a potential solution to the problem of cover – is to use video technology to record lessons for later viewing. Whatever method is used to observe lessons, it should be made clear that observations are not high stakes, graded observations. Indeed, because the lessons have been co-planned, there should be less fear and more trust built into the process. Also, the foci of observation are the case study pupils rather than the teacher.

Thirdly, the case study pupils are interviewed in order to gain an insight into their responses to the activity. A discussion is held with the research group to analyse how pupils have responded to the teaching strategy, what progress they have made, what they found difficult and what can be learned about how to develop the teaching strategy further.

Finally, the outcomes are shared with a wider audience (perhaps the whole department or staff).

Here are some useful questions for each stage…

Planning the lesson:
- Which member of the group will observe which pupil?
- What should the pupils be able to do by the end of the lesson? How will we know?

Reviewing the lesson:
- Was the research question answered? If so, how do we know? If not, why not?
- Did the pupils achieve what we predicted they would? If not, did they achieve more or less and why?
- What further actions do we now need to take?

Asking pupils to evaluate the lesson:
- What did you learn in the lesson and how do you know?
- What do you need to do next in order to build on that learning? What's the next step?
- What aspect(s) of the lesson worked well and what could have been improved? Why?

End Matter

M J Bromley

Conclusion

We're almost at the end of our journey now but, before we reach our final destination, let's recap on some of the important lessons we've learnt and consider what it is we're trying to achieve during our early years of teaching. What does our final product look like? And how can we evolve from a novice caterpillar into an expert butterfly..?

Pass the teaching test

Being a new teacher is a bit like learning to drive: throughout your teacher-training and induction you have a constant critic at your side offering advice (or possibly a staffroom full of them), and you are encouraged to endlessly reflect, adjust and - by so doing - secure incremental improvements. You might literally be in the driving seat but it sometimes it can feel like you're just along for the ride, following someone else's roadmap.

But once you've passed your test, so to speak, you'll be free to do it your way. You'll be a qualified, fully-fledged teacher with all the professional autonomy that goes with it. But be cautious...

Often, when people pass their driving tests, they begin undoing all their hard work, unlearning all the skills they acquired under the tutelage of their instructor. They stop holding the wheel at ten-to-two, stop changing down through the gears, and stop mirror-signal-manoeuvring.

Be careful not to let your teaching fall into the same trap: don't undo all the hard work you put in as an NQT and RQT and don't ever stop reflecting and improving. Don't start acquiring bad habits, cutting corners, and letting standards slide. Rather, add light and water to your blossoming career; grow into the expert teacher you know you're capable of being by building upon what you've already learnt through studying and practising your trade. Do not rest on your laurels; rather, learn and practice some more.

Expert teachers

So what are you practising for? What are you striving to become?

What exactly does it mean to be an expert teacher? David Berliner researched the nature of expertise in teaching and devised eight characteristics:

1. **Expert teachers excel mainly in their own domain**. That is to say a teacher who is effective at teaching A Levels might not be so effective at teaching Key Stage 3 or teaching pupils with special educational needs. So decide on your domain and become an expert in it.

2. **Expert teachers develop automaticity** for the regular routines and actions they perform in the classroom. In other words, whereas new teachers might take several hours to plan a lesson, an expert teacher could plan the lesson more effectively in just a matter of minutes. Berliner says expert teachers can be as much as fifty times faster at planning lessons than a newly qualified teacher.

There is no shortcut to this; automaticity comes with experience - but the more you practice, the better you'll become. So practice your regular classroom routines over and over until you perfect them and can perform them without much thought. Then concentrate your energies on the actions that will have the biggest impact on pupil learning. For example, the less time you spend on planning lessons, the more time you can spend on marking and giving feedback, or on developing quality classroom resources you can use time and again.

3. When solving problems, **expert teachers are more sensitive to the demands of the task** and to the social context. In other words, when asked to plan a lesson, expert teachers tend to want to know more information about the classroom in which they'll be teaching and about the starting points and backgrounds of the pupils they will be teaching than do newly qualified teachers.

So get to know the context in which you'll be teaching - do your research at the start of the new term, time spent on this will pay dividends throughout the year: know your pupils' starting points and backgrounds and use that information to inform your planning and teaching.

Again, the more you develop automaticity, the more time you'll have to look deeper at the contextual factors (such as your pupils' home-lives, interests, and preferred ways of learning) that might inform your teaching.

4. **Expert teachers are more flexible** in their approach than newly qualified teachers. Experts are more likely than new teachers to find solutions that are tailored to the particular circumstances rather than use a 'one size fits all' approach. They are also more likely to adapt their style and tone as a lesson progresses whereas new teachers tend to project the same emotions throughout a lesson.

Experience will breed comfort in the sense that, with practice, you will grow comfortable in your own skin as a teacher and become more willing to be yourself in the classroom, making emotional connections with your pupils without fear of compromising your authority. You will become less of an automaton and more human - adapting your style to suit the context.

5. Although new and experienced teachers do not differ in the amount of knowledge they have, they do differ in the way they organise that knowledge. In other words, new and expert teachers have similar levels of subject knowledge but **expert teachers have more pedagogical content knowledge**. For example, when describing a pupil, a new teacher is more likely to refer to personality whereas an expert is more likely to refer to learning needs.

As you grow with experience, you will learn how pupils respond to the subject content you teach them - what they tend to find easy and difficult, what they tend to need help with and what they can do independently. This will inform the way you teach that content in the future. You will get better at pre-empting pupil responses and so will plan for them.

6. **Expert teachers have faster and more accurate pattern recognition capabilities** than newly qualified teachers. In other words, new teachers cannot always make sense of their experiences. For example, a new teacher might not immediately recognise that a particular choice of classroom layout will prohibit the lesson they have planned whereas an expert teacher would.

Again, with practice, you will grow to understand how to organise learning. It will, eventually, become instinctual.

7. **Experts are also more skilled at deriving meaning from situations** with which they are familiar such as a classroom. For example, if you show a new teacher a picture of a classroom they might note that "pupils are sitting at a table" or perhaps "a group task is taking place in a science lab", whereas an expert teacher would discern which pupils are attentive and engaged and which are not, as well as what the classroom layout, group composition and learning materials - classroom displays and so on - are contributing to the lesson. This skill will help you understand what your pupils are doing and why. This will help you to 'read' your classroom more easily and quickly so you can adjust to the 'here and now' circumstances of your lessons.

8. Finally, **expert teachers take longer to begin solving a problem** than new teachers but do so in a richer and deeper way. For example, when asked to plan to meet the needs of a particular pupil, new teachers begin planning quickly whereas experts take longer to begin the planning process.

In a study carried out by Berliner, he found that new teachers took about three minutes to begin planning whereas experts took ten minutes. Expert teachers take longer to begin planning because they work through previous experiences to identify a situation they have already dealt with that is similar and then examine whether it is sufficiently similar for it to provide a useful guide. Just as pupils learn better when they connect new concepts to their prior learning, you too will become a better teacher the more background knowledge you acquire and the more connections you can make between experiences.

Expert teaching

If that's what it means to be an expert *teacher*, what does expert *teaching* look like? Well, there is no silver bullet, no secret formula to teaching expert lessons – what works is what's best. The best thing to do, therefore, is to get to know your pupils by regularly assessing them and then to plan for progress by providing opportunities for all your pupils to fill the gaps in their knowledge.

A lesson does not exist in isolation; it is all about context, so it is better to think of a lesson as one learning episode in a long series. It does not necessarily need a neat beginning and end or to be in four parts, and it does not need to prescribe to a particular style of teaching. For example, every lesson does not need to include opportunities for group work or independent study. A lesson can be meaningfully spent with pupils reading or writing in silence so long as, in the wider context of the series, there is a variety of learning activities.

The best teachers are sensitive to the needs of their pupils and adjust their lessons to the here and now. Pupils work best for the teachers who respect them, know their subjects, and are approachable, and enthusiastic. The most effective teachers are relentless in their pursuit of excellence and are able to explain complex concepts in a way which makes sense.

Pupils are more likely to get better at something if they believe intelligence can be changed through hard work. As such, the word 'yet' can be a powerful instrument in the teacher's toolbox: "I can't do this...yet" and "I don't understand this...yet" turn a pupil's negativity on its head and point to the importance of practice and perseverance. 'Yet' can also help build resilience.

The best classrooms are those in which pupils feel welcomed, valued, enthusiastic, engaged, and eager to experiment and rewarded for hard work. The way to achieve this is to prize effort over attainment and focus on progress not raw outcomes.

When planning lessons, we should focus on what pupils will be made to think about rather than on what they will do. We might, for example, organise a lesson around a big question. We then need to repeat learning several times – at least three times according to Graham Nuthall – if it is to penetrate pupils' long-term memories.

Tests interrupt forgetting and reveal what has actually been learnt as well as what gaps exist. Accordingly, we should run pre-tests at the start of every unit – perhaps as a multiple choice quiz – which will provide cues and improve subsequent learning. Retrieval activities like this also help pupils prepare for exams.

Classroom discussion – best achieved through artful questioning – makes pupils smarter because they make pupils think. Questions should only be used if they cause thinking and/or provide information for the teacher about what to do next (as such, it's best to avoid the 'guess what's in my head' charade).

The most common model of teacher talk is *IRE*: initiation, response, evaluation. But it doesn't work very well. A better model is *ABC*: agree/disagree with, build upon, and challenge whereby pupils pass questions around the classroom. The Japanese call this neriage which means 'to polish' – pupils polish each other's answers, refining them, challenging each other's thinking.

Increasing 'wait time' – the amount of time the teacher waits for an answer to their question before either answering it themselves or asking someone else – makes pupils' answers longer, more confident, and increases pupils' ability to respond.

Feedback works best when it is explicit about the marking criteria, offers suggestions for improvement, and is focused on how pupils can close the gap between their current performance and their desired performance; it does not focus on presentation or quantity of work.

Feedback can promote the growth mindset if it: is as specific as possible; focuses on factors within pupils' control; focuses on factors which are dependent on effort not ability; and motivates rather than frustrates pupils.

The only useful feedback is that which is acted upon – it is crucial that the teacher knows the pupil and knows when and what kind of feedback to give, then plans time for pupils to act on feedback.

The best way to develop a learning culture in which pupils produce high quality work is to set assignments which inspire and challenge pupils, and which are predicated on the idea of every pupil succeeding. You can also create an ethic of excellence by developing a sense of whole-class pride in the quality of learning and by ensuring that, once finished, assignments are made public –

providing the work with a genuine audience.

Assessments – such as gallery critique – should be used as a primary context for sharing knowledge and skills. To do this, you need to teach pupils how to give constructive feedback that is kind, helpful and specific, and you need to provide pupils with exemplars that show them what a great essay or experiment looks like.

Finally, expert teaching is achieved when you instil in pupils the belief that quality means rethinking, reworking, and polishing so that they feel celebrated, not ridiculed, for going back to the drawing board.

And the same principle applies to your teaching…

Don't ever forget - particularly in your darkest hours when you think you've made a massive mistake training to be a teacher; after all, there are easier ways to pay the mortgage - that teaching is a complex, nuanced art form concerned with the human interaction between you, the teacher, and your pupils, and with the connection that you make possible between the pupils in your classroom.

As such, sometimes things will go wrong. Sometimes, one of the thirty or so other human beings in your room may do or say something they shouldn't, or not say or do something they should. And sometimes you, as a human being with all the fallibility that that brings, may also make a mistake.

So what? That's life. Learn from it and bounce back from it. Resilience is a teacher's superpower. Harness it and use it for good. Model it. Share it. Pass it on. To quote Hector in Alan Bennett's play, The History Boys, "That's sometimes all you can do. Take it, feel it, and pass it on. Not for me, not for you, but for someone, somewhere, one day. Pass it on, boys. That's the game I want you to learn. Pass it on."

Good luck!

Bibliography and Further Reading

From Chapter One - Your first steps, Chapter Two - Surviving and thriving each term, and Chapter Three - Passing your induction year

NQT advice article - the habits of a great teacher:
http://www.sec-ed.co.uk/best-practice/nqt-special-the-habits-of-a-great-teacher/

The Teachers' Standards:
https://www.gov.uk/government/publications/teachers-standards

Information about the Teachers' Standards:
https://www.gov.uk/government/publications/teachers-standards

How to use The Teachers' Standards:
https://www.gov.uk/government/publications/teachers-standards

Initial Teacher Training info:
https://www.gov.uk/government/collections/initial-teacher-training

Advice for new teachers:

http://newteachers.tes.co.uk/teaching-tips

http://www.theguardian.com/teacher-network/teacher-blog/2013/sep/03/nqt-10-commandments-new-teachers

http://www.theguardian.com/teacher-network/2015/oct/08/classroom-management-tips-new-teachers

http://theconversation.com/whats-so-hard-about-teaching-words-of-advice-for-new-teachers-56884

http://www.theguardian.com/teacher-network/2013/sep/07/nqt-survival-guide-teaching-tips

http://tdtrust.org/4-ways-to-become-an-outstanding-nqt-2

From Chapter Four - Developing a presence in the classroom, Chapter Five - Creating your learning environment, and Chapter Six - Managing your time

https://www.educationsupportpartnership.org.uk/research-reports

http://www.theguardian.com/teacher-network/teacher-blog/2013/jun/25/teacher-work-life-balance-stress-tips

http://www.teachprimary.com/learning_resources/view/teaching-tips-getting-a-work-life-balance

http://www.mindfulteachers.org/2014/02/striving-for-worklife-balance-5-great.html

From Chapter Seven - Schools, phases and stages

Types of school:
https://www.gov.uk/types-of-school

Early Years Foundation Stage info:
https://www.gov.uk/early-years-foundation-stage

Attendance and absence info:
https://www.gov.uk/school-attendance-absence

Discipline and exclusion info:
https://www.gov.uk/school-discipline-exclusions

School leaving age info:
https://www.gov.uk/know-when-you-can-leave-school

Safeguarding:
https://www.gov.uk/topic/schools-colleges-childrens-services/safeguarding-children

Behaviour:
https://www.gov.uk/topic/schools-colleges-childrens-services/school-behaviour-attendance

SEND:

https://www.gov.uk/topic/schools-colleges-childrens-services/special-educational-needs-disabilities

From Chapter Eight - Curriculum and qualifications

National Curriculum – home page:
https://www.gov.uk/government/collections/national-curriculum

By key stage:
https://www.gov.uk/government/collections/national-curriculum#curriculum-by-key-stages

Key stage 1 and 2 curriculum:
https://www.gov.uk/national-curriculum/key-stage-1-and-2

Key stage 3 and 4 curriculum:
https://www.gov.uk/national-curriculum/key-stage-3-and-4

Programmes of study by subject:
https://www.gov.uk/government/collections/national-curriculum#programmes-of-study-by-subject

Curriculum assessment:
https://www.gov.uk/government/collections/national-curriculum#curriculum-assessment

GCSE subject content:
https://www.gov.uk/government/collections/gcse-subject-content

AS and A Level subject content:
https://www.gov.uk/government/collections/gce-as-and-a-level-subject-content

Exams, testing and assessment info:
https://www.gov.uk/topic/schools-colleges-childrens-services/exams-testing-assessment

Key stage 1 assessment and reporting arrangements:
https://www.gov.uk/guidance/2016-key-stage-1-assessment-and-reporting-arrangements-ara

Key stage 2 assessment and reporting arrangements:
https://www.gov.uk/guidance/2016-key-stage-2-assessment-and-reporting-arrangements-ara

Scaled scores at key stage 1:
https://www.gov.uk/guidance/scaled-scores-at-key-stage-1

From Chapter Nine: - Accountability and inspection

Department for Education – home page:
https://www.gov.uk/government/organisations/department-for-education

School performance tables:
http://www.education.gov.uk/schools/performance

Inspections:
https://www.gov.uk/topic/schools-colleges-childrens-services/inspections

Safeguarding:
https://www.gov.uk/topic/schools-colleges-childrens-services/safeguarding-children

Behaviour:
https://www.gov.uk/topic/schools-colleges-childrens-services/school-behaviour-attendance

SEND:
https://www.gov.uk/topic/schools-colleges-childrens-services/special-educational-needs-disabilities

Regional schools commissioners:
https://www.gov.uk/government/organisations/schools-commissioners-group

Ofsted:
https://www.gov.uk/government/organisations/ofsted

Ofqual:

https://www.gov.uk/government/organisations/ofqual

From Chapter Ten - Strategies for classroom management

Some of the text in these chapters has been adapted from:

Teach by M J Bromley published by Autus Books in 2014 ISBN-13: 978-1500733308 / ISBN-10: 150073330X and is reproduced with kind permission, and

Teach 2 published by Autus Books in 2016 ISBN-13: 978-1533169945 / ISBN-10: 1533169942 reproduced with kind permission, and

A Teacher's Guide to Assessment published by Autus Books 2012 revised 2014 ISBN-13: 978-1480269613 / ISBN-10: 1480269611 reproduced with kind permission.

A Teacher's Guide to Behaviour Management by M J Bromley published by Autus Books 2012 (revised 2014) and is reproduced with kind permission. ISBN-13: 978-1478341451 / ISBN-10: 1478341459.

More useful reading:

https://www.tes.com/articles/tes-classroom-behaviour#.V2eohLsrIdU

https://www.tes.com/teaching-resource/top-10-behaviour-management-tips-3006435

https://mjbromleyblog.wordpress.com/2013/11/28/behaviour-advice-for-nqts/

http://www.teachprimary.com/learning_resources/view/behaviour-management-advice-for-nqts

http://www.behavioradvisor.com/oldindex.html

http://www.sec-ed.co.uk/best-practice/nqt-special-strategies-for-managing-behaviour/

http://www.theguardian.com/education/2012/aug/27/pupil-behaviour-management-teaching-resources

http://www.suecowley.co.uk/100-tips-on-behaviour.html

http://www.creativeeducation.co.uk/blog/free-advice-from-sue-cowley-on-behaviour-management/

https://www.theguardian.com/society/joepublic/2010/feb/09/pupil-behaviour-management-tips

https://headguruteacher.com/2013/01/06/behaviour-management-a-bill-rogers-top-10/

https://www.teachit.co.uk/user_content/satellites/6/schoolplacements/Behaviour%20management%20advice%20leaflet%20Feb%202010.pdf

http://mindsetonline.com/whatisit/about/

https://www.mindsetworks.com/webnav/whatismindset.aspx

http://www.edweek.org/ew/articles/2015/09/23/carol-dweck-revisits-the-growth-mindset.html

From Chapter Eleven - Dealing with common misbehaviours, and Chapter Twelve - Using rewards and sanctions

Some of the text in this email is adapted from A Teacher's Guide to Behaviour Management by M J Bromley published by Autus Books 2012 (revised 2014) and is reproduced with kind permission. ISBN-13: 978-1478341451 / ISBN-10: 1478341459.

More behaviour management advice:

https://www.tes.com/articles/tes-classroom-behaviour#.V2eohLsrIdU

https://www.tes.com/teaching-resource/top-10-behaviour-management-tips-3006435

https://mjbromleyblog.wordpress.com/2013/11/28/behaviour-advice-for-nqts/

http://www.teachprimary.com/learning_resources/view/behaviour-management-advice-for-nqts

http://www.behavioradvisor.com/oldindex.html

http://www.sec-ed.co.uk/best-practice/nqt-special-strategies-for-managing-behaviour/

http://www.theguardian.com/education/2012/aug/27/pupil-behaviour-management-teaching-resources

http://www.suecowley.co.uk/100-tips-on-behaviour.html

http://www.creativeeducation.co.uk/blog/free-advice-from-sue-cowley-on-behaviour-management/

https://www.theguardian.com/society/joepublic/2010/feb/09/pupil-behaviour-management-tips

https://headguruteacher.com/2013/01/06/behaviour-management-a-bill-rogers-top-10/

https://www.teachit.co.uk/user_content/satellites/6/schoolplacements/Behaviour%20management%20advice%20leaflet%20Feb%2010.pdf

From Chapter Thirteen - Planning lessons

Some of the text in this chapter has been adapted from:

Teach 2 published by Autus Books in 2016 ISBN-13: 978-1533169945 / ISBN-10: 1533169942 reproduced with kind permission, and

A Teacher's Guide to Assessment published by Autus Books 2012 revised 2014 ISBN-13: 978-1480269613 / ISBN-10: 1480269611 reproduced with kind permission.

More useful reading:

Lesson planning:

https://newteachers.tes.co.uk/news/realistic-guide-lesson-planning/45965

http://www.sec-ed.co.uk/best-practice/five-keys-to-learning-grabbing-pupils-attention/

http://www.sec-ed.co.uk/best-practice/eight-steps-to-teaching-excellence/

http://www.sec-ed.co.uk/best-practice/nqt-special-best-laid-lesson-plans/

Starters and plenary activities.

https://outstanding-lessons.wikispaces.com/Starters+and+Plenaries

http://teacherrebootcamp.com/2012/08/18/the-teachers-survival-kit-for-lesson-planning-tips-1000s-of-free-lesson-plans/

Marking:

http://www.theguardian.com/teacher-network/teacher-blog/2012/dec/03/five-ways-reduce-stress-marking-teaching-tips

http://www.sec-ed.co.uk/best-practice/giving-effective-pupil-feedback/

http://www.theguardian.com/teacher-network/teacher-blog/2014/apr/16/how-to-marking-techniques-teacher-feedback-pupils

https://newteachers.tes.co.uk/news/advice-most-effective-way-mark-homework/45934

https://newteachers.tes.co.uk/news/importance-marking/45966

From Chapter Fourteen - Establishing high expectations, and Chapter Fifteen - The importance of high expectations

Some of the text in these chapters has been adapted from:

Teach by M J Bromley published by Autus Books in 2014 ISBN-13: 978-1500733308 / ISBN-10: 150073330X and is reproduced with kind permission, and

Teach 2 published by Autus Books in 2016 ISBN-13: 978-1533169945 / ISBN-10: 1533169942 reproduced with kind permission, and

A Teacher's Guide to Assessment published by Autus Books 2012 revised 2014 ISBN-13: 978-1480269613 / ISBN-10: 1480269611 reproduced with kind permission.

More useful reading:

http://www.johnbiggs.com.au/academic/constructive-alignment/

http://www.learningandteaching.info/learning/solo.htm

http://pamhook.com/solo-taxonomy/

http://www.johnbiggs.com.au/academic/solo-taxonomy/

http://www.ascd.org/ASCD/pdf/journals/ed_lead/el_198809_perkins.pdf

https://howthebrainlearns.wordpress.com/2012/01/23/teaching-for-transfer/

http://www.sec-ed.co.uk/best-practice/giving-effective-pupil-feedback/

The traits of a master teacher pt1:
http://www.sec-ed.co.uk/best-practice/the-traits-of-the-master-teacher/

The traits of a master teacher pt2:
http://www.sec-ed.co.uk/best-practice/the-traits-of-the-master-teacher/

What makes great teaching? – A review of the underpinning research from The Sutton Trust:
http://www.suttontrust.com/wp-content/uploads/2014/10/What-makes-great-teaching-FINAL-4.11.14.pdf

From Chapter Sixteen - Marking, Chapter Seventeen - Giving feedback, and Chapter Eighteen - Using comment-only feedback

Some of the text in this chapter has been adapted from:

Teach by M J Bromley published by Autus Books in 2014 ISBN-13: 978-1500733308 / ISBN-10: 150073330X and is reproduced with kind permission, and

Teach 2 published by Autus Books in 2016 ISBN-13: 978-1533169945 / ISBN-10: 1533169942 reproduced with kind permission, and

A Teacher's Guide to Assessment published by Autus Books 2012 revised 2014 ISBN-13: 978-1480269613 / ISBN-10: 1480269611 reproduced with kind permission.

More useful reading:

https://mjbromleyblog.wordpress.com/2015/12/02/is-teaching-as-simple-as-abc/

https://mjbromleyblog.wordpress.com/2014/05/17/growth-mindset/

https://mjbromleyblog.wordpress.com/2014/07/06/outstanding-teaching-what-i-really-think/

http://bjorklab.psych.ucla.edu/research.html

https://www.psychologytoday.com/blog/all-about-addiction/201105/desirable-difficulties-in-the-classroom

http://www.simplypsychology.org/Zone-of-Proximal-Development.html

http://www.learnnc.org/lp/pages/5075

https://www.cmu.edu/teaching/assessment/basics/formative-summative.html

http://www.journeytoexcellence.org.uk/videos/expertspeakers/formativeassessmentdylanwiliam.asp

http://ccea.org.uk/curriculum/assess_progress/types_assessment/formative/assessment_learning

http://www.ed.ac.uk/institute-academic-development/learning-teaching/staff/advice/assessment/resources/principles

From Chapter Nineteen - Being a form tutor

http://www.theguardian.com/teacher-network/2015/aug/26/six-basic-steps-brilliant-form-tutor

http://www.sec-ed.co.uk/best-practice/top-tips-for-tutor-time/

https://newteachers.tes.co.uk/news/sixth-form-tutor-maintaining-balance/45769

https://newteachers.tes.co.uk/news/tutors-should-be-top-form/45765

From Chapter Twenty - The SEND code *of* practice, and Chapter Twenty-One - The SEND code *in* practice

https://www.gov.uk/government/publications/send-code-of-practice-0-to-25

http://www.specialneedsjungle.com/code-practice-look-like-schools/

http://www.sendgateway.org.uk/resources.special-educational-needs-and-disability-code-of-practice-0-to-25-years.html

https://www.gov.uk/government/publications/teaching-pupils-with-special-educational-needs-and-disabilities-send

https://www.gov.uk/children-with-special-educational-needs/overview

http://www.ase.org.uk/resources/send/

From Chapter Twenty-Two - Child protection, Chapter Twenty-Three - Your legal duties, and Chapter Twenty-Four - Health and safety

https://www.gov.uk/government/publications/safeguarding-in-schools-best-practice

https://www.gov.uk/government/uploads/system/uploads/attachment_data/file/417715/Archived-Keeping_children_safe_in_education.pdf

https://www.nspcc.org.uk/preventing-abuse/safeguarding/schools-protecting-children-abuse-neglect/

https://www.nspcc.org.uk/preventing-abuse/safeguarding/

From Chapter Twenty-Five - Making the most of INSET, Chapter Twenty-Six - Coaching and mentoring, and Chapter Twenty-Seven - Video and lesson study

http://tdtrust.org/what-is-lesson-study

http://lessonstudy.co.uk/

http://teachmeet.pbworks.com/w/page/19975349/FrontPage

http://inservice.ascd.org/peer-to-peer-observation-five-questions-for-making-it-work/

http://www.ascd.org/publications/educational-leadership/may14/vol71/num08/Rethinking-Classroom-Observation.aspx

http://wp.me/P3roL1-dR

https://educationechochamber.wordpress.com/2016/01/10/list-of-uk-education-blogs-version-13-2/

https://educationechochamber.wordpress.com/2015/01/08/where-to-find-education-bloggers-on-twitter-version-4-0/

About the author

Matt Bromley is an experienced education leader, writer, consultant, speaker and trainer.

You can find out more about him and read his free blog at
www.bromleyeducation.co.uk

You can follow him on Twitter
@mj_bromley

Also by the author

Leadership for Learning
Ofsted Thriving Not Surviving
A Teacher's Guide to Outstanding Lessons
A Teacher's Guide to Assessment
A Teacher's Guide to Behaviour Management
The Art of Public Speaking
How to Become a School Leader
Teach
School of Thoughts
Teach 2: Educated Risks
Making Key Stage 3 Count

As Editor
SPaG Book (by Matilda Rose)
Outstanding Literacy (by Matilda Rose)

Published by Spark Education Books UK
Twitter: @SparkBooksUK

Published in 2017
© Bromley Education 2017

The right of M J Bromley to be identified as the author of this work has been asserted by him in accordance with the Copyrights, Designs and Patents Act 1988

ISBN-13: 978-1542815932
ISBN-10: 1542815932

Printed in Great Britain
by Amazon